Authoritarian Collectivism
and 'Real Socialism'

T0352466

Authoritarian Collectivism and 'Real Socialism'

Twentieth-Century Trajectory, Twenty-First Century Issues

José Maurício Domingues

ANTHEM PRESS

Anthem Press
An imprint of Wimbledon Publishing Company
www.anthempress.com

This edition first published in UK and USA 2022
by ANTHEM PRESS
75–76 Blackfriars Road, London SE1 8HA, UK
or PO Box 9779, London SW19 7ZG, UK
and
244 Madison Ave #116, New York, NY 10016, USA

British Library Cataloguing-in-Publication Data
A catalogue record for this book is available from the British Library.

Library of Congress Control Number: 2021951237

ISBN-13: 978-1-83998-077-0 (Pbk)
ISBN-10: 1-83998-077-X (Pbk)

Cover Image: Soviet red propaganda poster of the Cold War, raised in the air fist,
sickle and the star of communism. THE USSR, by Andrew1998 / Shutterstock.com

This title is also available as an e-book.

CONTENTS

INTRODUCTION

The goal of this short book is to discuss what the purportedly socialist societies of the twentieth century were, and what is left of them at present. I approach these societies starting from a specific entry point, that is, I focus on the political dimension, which I elaborate on below, which allows for a broader characterization of the topic. I call the sort of social system discussed here 'authoritarian collectivism'. It was based on the party-state structure and democratic centralism and was structured as a *system of rule*. Generally, it did not survive into the twenty-first century, though, in some cases, the specific political dimension and partly its state were retained with the transition to a variant of capitalism in which citizens' rights remain secondary, thus reproducing the former framework. This was a strategy of adaptation implemented once the system evolutionarily proved too fragile to reform. The political system at its core found a new lease of life in combination with a sort of state-based capitalism, reminiscent of a prior phase of modernity – state-organized – with which the so-called 'real socialism' had important affinities. It was then perhaps that this sort of social system more clearly revealed how distant it was from socialism proper, despite the use of the word 'socialism' to define it.

The use of the political catchphrase 'real socialism' (also 'really/actually existing socialism' – *real existierender Sozialismus*) in this book requires a brief explanation, though this is obviously a rather current expression. It was originally coined by Erich Honecker, the general secretary of the East German Socialist Unity Party (SED), in 1973. It paralleled Leonid Brezhnev's introduction of the idea of 'developed socialism', also in the 1970s (Sandle 2002). Even though the expression has perhaps a less optimistic ring to it, Honecker coined it as a sort of praise for the society he saw his country as concretely embodying. Afterwards, it was applied in a critical way, rather diffusely, to conceptualize the social system of the Soviet Union and the countries that basically followed its model. That is, while the original coinage implied an actual definition of the concrete model of socialism that would have been built in these countries, others would use it to disqualify them as socialist, or point out how distorted the model was, mostly due to authoritarianism. I will at times refer to authoritarian collectivism as 'real socialism', using the term as a native category, without ever implying that these countries were socialist, irrespective of how deeply many people, within and without, as well as their rulers believed that they were building socialism and preparing the ground for communism. To be sure, the people, cadres and militants, rulers and ideologues, in each of these countries, starting with the Soviet Union and later in Eastern Europe and the Balkans, in Asia, Latin America and Africa, developed their societies according to specific historic circumstances and to some extent creatively, with all the positive and negative aspects of this attempt at superseding capitalism. Yet the pristine Soviet model, especially after it was stabilized and had shed Stalinist terror, was, in one way or another, reproduced, regardless of how state and regime were defined. It is the main traits of this model, along with the treatment of some national particularities, that form the focus of this book. This system was indeed postmodern, but did not configure a socialist society, as I shall argue throughout the book.

I must also comment on the relation between history and the analytical exposition I articulate in these pages. I have tried to flesh this relation out and account for some variation in the implementation of authoritarian collectivism as a system of rule in specific contexts. The model as such, exported afterwards, stems from the Soviet experience, especially from the 1930s onwards. How revolution and authoritarian collectivism were established did depend on concrete historical circumstances and political inventiveness to some extent, within the limits set by political ruling circles. However, the new society was to a large extent at variance with the basic model and mould that Marxism had imagined for socialism once the revolutionaries came to power and then built it, although they did follow some of Marx and Engels' recommendations, as we shall see. If capitalism found its original paradigmatic instance in nineteenth-century England, collective authoritarianism had the Soviet Union as its chief reference. This underpins the framework that I try to articulate here as a theoretical exercise, without forgetting history and contingency. In my exposition, I will therefore work first on the principal analytical categories of authoritarian collectivism, moving then to its developmental dynamics. Finally, I will tackle its contemporary changes, including a glance at future possibilities.

An underlying concern of this book is the validity and possibility of socialism as a *horizon of possibilities*, which must to a large extent be unprecedented – especially in view of its historical failure in the guise of 'real socialism' or, as I prefer to name it, *authoritarian collectivism*. There has been a tense dialogue and sometimes fierce exchange between liberalism, not to speak of fascism, and socialism, including communism. Socialism and communism craved to leave modernity behind, replacing it with a truly 'emancipated' society. How it turned out in practice is what I investigate here; for, to unlock the future, it is important to consider what happened to the project of an emancipated society which socialism or communism – as well as anarchism – strived to bring about, notwithstanding the present improbability of effective movements in what regards the construction of a socialist society.

I thank the National Research Council (CNPq) of the Brazilian Ministry of Science, Technology and Innovation, the Rio de Janeiro State Research Foundation (FAPERJ) and the Alexander von Humboldt Stiftung in Germany, from which I received the Anneliese Maier Research Award in 2018, for their support in researching for this book. I would also like to thank Leander Badura for his research assistance and Clay Johnson for his revision of the text, as well as Anthem's anonymous reviewers and staff.

Chapter 1

AUTHORITARIAN COLLECTIVISM AND THE POLITICAL DIMENSION

We live in a postsocialist world. Surely, some states still call themselves 'socialist' and pretend to be moving towards communism – even if, taking a step back and evincing greater modesty, their stage of 'socialism' would correspond to its first and protracted phase. Many others across the world used to call themselves 'socialist'. This should not, however, lead us to accept their postulation, formerly or today, no more than we should take any individuals according to their own evaluation or capitalists according to what they think of themselves (see Marx [1859] 1971). Yet, if they were not 'socialist', what were they?

Socialism, let alone communism, cannot be authoritarian – even if we could accept a rather quick stage of the 'dictatorship of proletariat' – nor should it be seen as a sort of collectivism. On the other hand, state property of the 'means of production' in and by itself does not make a country socialist. Democracy – which must be based on equal and free positions and mostly horizontal relations – as well as the flourishing of individuality, without detriment to collective well-being, both have to stand out in any social formation that deserves the name of socialism, with its implications for truly social, collectively shared property. This was not the case of authoritarian collectivism, even though not everything that developed therein was bad or negative (with the caveat that positivity was often wrapped in some sort of state paternalism). Nor does recognizing the infirmity of 'real socialism' deny the sincere beliefs of members of such societies, including in many cases those sitting at the top, foremost but not only their founding fathers. We must not, of course, forget the role of ideologies as well as that of flawed knowledge in the only partial grasp they had of their own reality, but this does not imply insincerity. In any case, socialism in the twentieth century did not set out with an authoritarian blueprint. The Bolsheviks, in particular, were, despite fierce debates about the role of centralization, largely a democratic and open party, a model they apparently projected onto the future socialist/communist society (Rabinowitch

1976, 2007). How this came to be so radically altered does not have an obvious answer.

Searching for a renewed conceptualization, my focus here is on the political dimension and political command (an essential feature of hierarchy) of these formerly postcapitalist, authoritarian collectivist societies, which has been partly carried over in the transition back to capitalism.[1] The political dimension was the dominant aspect of these societies and it is there that its problems of legitimation were most clearly felt, although speaking of a 'Jacobin dictatorship' hardly makes sense (Fehér, Heller and Márkus 1983, ch. 1, 56–57, 60, 70, 139ff.; Tarifa 1998).[2] This is an argument with, at most, allusive and polemical force regarding the concentration of power that came about in these systems of rule. It was in fact a radicalization, in this regard remaining largely parasitical, of the political aspects of modernity which characterizes authoritarian collectivism – and particularly political command, as elaborated below – in spite of its development as a separate civilization. We therefore need to concentrate both substantively and methodologically on the political dimension, taking into account its entanglement with 'ideology', that is to say, with how legitimation worked through the imaginary of these societies. They were heavily charged with 'Marxist-Leninist' tenets and promises regarding socialism and communism which could not be fulfilled. Especially, political ideology was crucial in the genesis and, in another vein, the functioning of these postmodern societies. I shall add reasons for my definition of the political dimension as representing the dominant element of these societies throughout the text, although, except for dogmatic understandings of Marxism and their concentration on the 'economic basis', this should no longer be necessary.

If the Soviet Union and Eastern Europe embraced modernity more straightforwardly since 1989, including capitalism and some form of the modern state and political regime, other countries have held fast to that specific political dimension and core. They encompass a huge part of the world, beginning with the People's Republic of China, but including also Vietnam, Laos, North Korea and Cuba as well as at least partly Angola and Mozambique. Understanding them today requires a good grasp, too, of what they were before. I try to give some attention, especially through the specialized bibliography, to all these cases. But the Soviet Union stands out in the book in that it was the first country to build 'real socialism', and because it exported its model worldwide, even if there were divergences between its ruling circles and those of other authoritarian collectivist countries. China gains prominence in the exposition as we approach the present, in that it is the main exemplar of a successful reconciliation of the political structure of collective authoritarianism with revived and renewed forms of capitalism.

The political dimension did not exist before modernity. Power has always, in any civilization, evidently been a key feature of social life, more or less equally or unequally distributed, and decision-making processes regularly occurred, including those associated with the state, which pre-existed the political dimension proper. They are always a feature of whatever civilization or specific social formations, with differentiations therein which are not the same as those that characterize modernity. It is among these provinces that we find – in modernity – the political dimension, one in which the exercise of power and decision-making processes that affect the whole society take place, with an interplay between state and society centred around the former and a corresponding logic (Domingues 2019a).

Modernity recognized naked power possibly for the first time in history – Machiavelli is often credited with this discovery. Liberalism immediately tried then to depoliticize politics, in whose core power would not be present. The mere defence of previously given rights should be pursued by a neutral and pacifying state, with however an inevitably conflictive political dynamic ensuing henceforth and making of liberalism a much more complex historical reality. Socialism, communism, anarchism and similar doctrines, initially stemming from the perceived limitations of liberalism and emergent social struggles, were meant to change all this, even if they had no clear blueprint for the future. While social democracy accommodated itself consciously and willingly to modernity – to the state, law and rights – those other perspectives and movements envisaged a sort of postmodern society in which power would be equally distributed and a political dimension as such would no longer exist, whatever this was supposed to mean, the 'administration of things' rather than 'domination over men' often being voiced as their goal. State and law would disappear, freedom for each and every one would set in.

Indeed, a postmodern type of society did emerge in the twentieth century as an attempt to embody these ideals and projects. Modernity, it should be remembered, is characterized by a number of features, including capitalism and the modern, basically liberal state, as well as a sort of nuclear family. If authoritarian collectivism radicalized some aspects of the modern state, as we shall see below, capitalism was discarded and even the liberal aspects of the modern state were still, albeit very selectively, taken up. Its imaginary was radically different too, with notions of freedom, equality and solidarity taking on very different meanings from those they evince in modernity, even if its relation with 'nature' was the same as that of modernity's, that is, it was an object simply to be exploited for the benefit of humanity.

Authoritarian collectivism was therefore neither anti-modern, in that it saw itself as superseding modernity in a simple evolutionary line, nor a self-destructive version of modernity (Arnason 1993). If it resumed archaic tsarist practices (without necessarily implying 'cultural' commitments, pragmatism as to solutions easily pushing in this direction) in the Soviet Union and other traditions elsewhere, it still thought of itself as a radically novel social formation, which it was indeed, though it was not socialist. It evinced grave shortcomings and had serious trouble competing with its entrenched modern enemies, but it was not an 'alternative' sort of modernity either (Sakwa 2013), as it departed from it in several ways, and parasitically (though also to some extent inevitably) took over many of its imaginary and institutional elements, as 'revolutionary' societies (Sweezy 1980). Something new historically and evolutionarily, which was neither socialism nor communism, much less anarchism, despite the initial aspirations of those who inadvertently brought it about, crept out of the revolutionary processes. It changed the differentiation of society – imaginarily and institutionally – but attributed absolute paramountcy to the political dimension, which it transplanted from modernity, with this specific dimension now subordinating virtually everything else.

While the debate about 'real socialism' was rather extensive, it was also often superficial, Cold War–oriented or reflected very dogmatic and polemical disputes within the Left. It would not be of great interest to pursue its analysis here as this has been done elsewhere by a number of authors, with distinct political and theoretical orientations (see Carlo [1971] 1975, part I; Cohen 1985, ch. 1; Linden 1992; Arato 1993; Lipset and Bence 1994). In general, the richest bibliography refers to the Soviet Union, then to China (with some Orientalist culturalism), less consistently to Eastern Europe (Hungary, Czechoslovakia and Poland) as well as Yugoslavia, Cuba and Vietnam. It is sketchier or focuses on more specific issues regarding other countries in the Balkans (Bulgaria, Romania and Albania), Indochina (Laos and Cambodia) and Africa (Angola and Mozambique), let alone Yemen. Most of this literature is not always terribly interesting and not much of it is theoretical, though notions such as 'totalitarianism', 'state capitalism', 'bureaucracy' and the like do inform the more circumscribed analyses.

In order to understand the specific features and dynamics of such societies in greater depth, I will mainly draw upon the more theoretically oriented literature and in the process propose a number of concepts under which they can all be subsumed. These concepts are put forward in analytical terms, replicating in a condensed way the Hegelian–Marxist method of exposition (Hegel [1820] 1986; Marx, [1867] 1962; Domingues 2019a), with a focus on the political dimension, which encompasses, especially in this case, the juridical aspect. Let us now review the main conceptualizations of 'real socialism' (beyond the traditional Trotskyist conception of the Soviet Union as a 'degenerate workers' state', to which I shall return later on, and other similar Marxist polemics, including the implausible idea of 'state capitalism' for such societies in the twentieth century, in which no private property of the 'means of production' existed).

The idea of 'collectivism' appears for the first time as a reference to a new system of domination in Rizzi's ([1939] 1976) somewhat odd book, which points to a new bureaucratic layer that eventually subordinated the working class. It implied a new 'central political bureaucracy' or 'ruling bureaucratic class', as Carlo ([1971] 1975, 70–110) and Melotti (1972, 50–51, 214–35) would, respectively, later put it, critically resuming Rizzi's ideas (Carlo more sympathetic towards China, Melotti connecting bureaucratic collectivism historically to the former weight of the 'Asiatic mode of production' in the East). 'Central political bureaucracy', an idea that will also be displayed in this book, though rendered with somewhat different words, is an expression Carlo took from Kuron and Modzelewski's ([1966] 1982, 15) (at the time still neo-Marxist) attack on the Polish party bureaucracy in its version of 'real socialism'. While Rizzi was innovative, he included the whole world in a vision of general bureaucratization and merely provided a conceptual sketch; furthermore, his book went basically unheeded, while Eastern European critics slowly found a broader yet arguably limited audience in the West. In any case, it was basically with Castoriadis (1990), in the mid-1940s, starting from within Trotskyist debates, that the idea of a new social formation, a novel and unanticipated type of society or civilization, was theoretically consolidated, still within a Marxist framework. Except in France, his ideas do not seem to have had a great impact on the discussion.

Castoriadis focused on the difference between formal, juridical property relations and actual property relations (of *possession*) as well as on the exploitative and 'parasitical' character of the bureaucracy, which would be incapable of developing the productive forces (within which he occasionally referred to the whole system as 'bureaucratic capitalism'). The formal, juridical relations establishing state ownership over the means of production actually served as a convenient cover for the bureaucracy's 'collective private ownership' of the means of production (Castoriadis [1947] 1990, 73). This was a rather problematic argument for a society that hardly knew the distinction between 'public' and 'private' (a point to which I will return later). Moreover, while Castoriadis did not miss the centrality of the political dimension as such, he did analytically and explicitly conflate bureaucracy and hierarchical political power (they were in fact 'fused', he argued – Castoriadis [1947] 1990, 74), losing sight of *political hierarchy* as the defining issue, in addition to more properly opposing such hierarchies to workers' horizontal self-management. The very genesis of Bolshevik/Communist power was not the genesis of bureaucratic power, he wrongly suggested (following Leon Trotsky, despite strong criticisms that bring out the authoritarianism shared by the main tribune of the 1905 and 1917 Russian revolutions) (Castoriadis [1964] 1973). Castoriadis would eventually abandon Marxism, but would seemingly retain the hypothesis of bureaucratic parasitism.[3]

Lefort ([1960] 1971), a former collaborator of Castoriadis in the group *Socialisme et barbarie*, followed the same path, emphasizing the domination of the bureaucracy. Yet, like Trotsky, despite soon dismissing his thesis of the 'degenerate workers' state', Lefort was especially concerned with politics. Despite this, he curiously continued to stress bureaucratic (not really essentially political) domination. Both Castoriadis and Lefort therefore overlooked the crucial issue I have underlined: it was not bureaucratic command but political command that really counted in this sort of civilization.

It is necessary to be wary of Weber's ([1918] 1988) stress on the prospective role of bureaucracy in socialism as well, since he often blurred the border between political domination and bureaucracy (Weber [1921–22] 1980, 122–76). Not by chance do we find a similar confusion between bureaucracy and politics in Michels's ([1911] 1915, viii, 31-3-86, 205–9, 400–401) famous book on political parties, particularly German social democracy. He belonged to Weber's circle before the latter put forward his theses on bureaucracy, and his ideas are likely to have had a subterranean, hidden influence in the posterior analysis of 'real socialism' (subterranean particularly because Michels later aligned with Fascism – but see Drochon 2020 for further observations). The growth of the division of labour, a technical issue to which Michels gives great weight, as well as the 'greed' of leaders for power, their differentiated evolution within the organization (becoming a 'caste') and the 'passivity of the masses' were the elements that explained the inevitable oligarchization of political organizations through bureaucratization. Although these are accurate arguments, it is hardly tenable to derive political power simply from bureaucratic complexity and so strongly stress the political incapacity of ordinary workers (which is at least in some part an outcome of oligarchization).

It is indeed remarkable that so many Marxists and post/former Marxists since Trotsky embraced the same sort of reasoning, evincing a central issue in the development of modernity – bureaucratization – and reflection on it. Interestingly, however, Castoriadis ([1948] 1990, 101–3) seems to have been the only one among them to stress the role of bureaucratic, *reified and abstract universalism*, which was a main concern for Weber ([1921–22] 1980). This is extremely important, though, again, it has to be tempered by an acknowledgement of the role of politics, which subordinated and sometimes undercut abstract universalism.

We need to be even more careful with the theory of totalitarianism, usually associated with Cold War Sovietology in the United States. Though this school of thought correctly pointed to the widespread intrusion of the state in social life and the role of propaganda and repression, its analytical capacity was very limited. This holds true whether we take Arendt's ([1951] 1973) rather loose book – based on Nazism, jumping, however, without mediation to the Soviet Union[4] – or the more sober approach of Friedrich and Brzezinski ([1956] 1963), which draws, however, the same absolutist and flat picture of politics and social life, even while stressing the role of the political system. Giddens (1985, 295ff.) put forward some crucial critical remarks regarding this sort of approach, stressing how much the capacity for surveillance and repression increasingly characterizes all modern states. Moreover, he more finely depicted the personalization of power, as well as the oligarchy and autocracy distinction as to political systems, than Friedrich and Brzezinski did.

Pluralism as a theory was more flexible and explicitly critical of the theories of totalitarianism, which it aimed to substitute. It stressed the flexibility of the Soviet Union as well as the complexity of its social life and the plurality of emerging interests therein. The authors who took this approach therefore offered a partial alternative to the theory of totalitarianism, though sometimes going too far in their effort to de-demonize the countries they studied (see Hough 1977; Solomon 1983; Harding 1984). In a way, that was Aron's ([1965] 2017) demarche too. Though he aligned with the theory of totalitarianism, in a Durkheimian fashion Aron pointed to the features of 'industrial society' that underlay both the 'pluralist-constitutional' (liberal) and the 'monopolistic party' regimes. The two responded to similar issues in different ways, with a high and encompassing politicization of the latter, centred on the Communist Party. A normalizing type of differentiation was increasingly present in the Soviet Union, though Aron stopped short of proposing a pluralist account of its political dynamic. Both systems might eventually, though partially, converge. Though less theoretically based, the idea that Stalinism was a 'revolution from above' (Tucker 1999), which unleashed huge amounts of violence and permanently satured the trajectory of authoritarian collectivism, must in any case be retained in a more pluralistic approach.

Within critical theory, the work of Fehér, Heller and Márkus (1983), Lukács's former students, offers the most systematic approach to 'Soviet type' societies. However, it overstates the putative rigidity of these countries and evinces a malaise explicable by the first-hand experience of oppression which these engaged intellectuals, once deeply committed to Marxism, had to endure. Nevertheless, I will often draw upon their approach, recognizing the problems they pointed out but surely more emotionally distanced than them. Other internal critical approaches include those such as Djilas's (1957), for whom the *party-state* as a system of politically based domination was the core of the problem, an issue which is dealt with, among others, by Bahro's (1977) critique of the *nomenklatura* as well.

Before getting into the thick of the argument, let me add a couple of concepts that underpin, on a general theoretical level, my approach. 'Institutions' as a concept is well sedimented in sociology, for instance in Durkheim and Parsons, roughly corresponding to Marx's 'social relations'. Conversely, the 'imaginary', in the form put forward here, positive and productive, rather than entailing something like alienation, derives to a large extent from Castoriadis and frameworks tributary to his ideas, though sociology and all the disciplines in the humanities (for instance, Marx, Durkheim, Freud, Weber, Mead, Saussure) have addressed and conceptualized the issue. I myself have synthetized these ideas (initially in Domingues 2000, ch. 2, and more recently in Domingues 2019a). The concept of institution refers to regularized patterns of behaviour of and interactions between individuals and between collectivities ('collective subjectivities'), the concept of imaginary to how the world is symbolically organized as well as to how individuals and collectivities create and make sense of the world. The former gives some stability to social life; the latter, with its floating, magmatic character, implies that the world is always somehow changing. Individual and collective practice mediates between them.

Chapter 2

POLITICAL COMMAND:
THE ELEMENTARY 'CELL-FORM'

For Marx ([1867] 1962, 12, 49) the commodity furnished the 'cell-form', the 'elementary' building block of the capitalist mode of production, as he stated in the opening chapter of *Capital*. The economic dimension being his focus, market relations, of which the commodity is the basic expression, played the decisive role, allowing for an initial analysis of the whole mode of production. It was based on 'voluntary exchange' (see below) and stood out in the articulation of capitalism. In authoritarian collectivism, it is the political dimension on which we must focus our attention. 'Command' can be found in any sort of social formation and in any dimension thereof (in the factory, in the family and so forth). In the case of authoritarian collectivism, it was *political command* that was key. Bureaucratic commands were ultimately subordinated to it, as they are subordinated to economic production and ultimately to market coordination within capitalist economic systems, as Marx ([1867] 1962, 350) himself showed in *Capital* with respect to capitalist firms. What characterizes command, and in particular political command?

Command is a *mechanism of coordination* of interactions. These interactions may be fleeting or they may endure, finding moorings in stable, regular relationships and rules/norms attached to them, also stabilizing otherwise tendentially free-floating imaginary, symbolic elements. This implies to a variable extent top-down connections between agents, which must usually find some sort of legitimation or justification. Command underpins *hierarchy* as a *principle of organization*, asymmetrical positioning within interactions, one in which agent A can *command* another agent, B, to do something, whether B is inclined and wants to do this or not (Domingues 2017/2018, ch. 7, 2019a, ch. 1).[1] That is, B must obey A's order. But so as to make sure and actually even define command as such – beyond more vague influence, suggestion and suchlike – it is necessary that A can actually force B to comply with, that is, to obey, A's demand. This is possible only if A can bring a sanction to bear on B's behaviour, if B is not willing to comply. This sanction, within market-oriented relations, can be an economic sanction – for instance, in a capitalist firm the worker may be fired, lose his or her wages or incur other indirect means of payment. In a bureaucratic setting it may be demotion to lesser positions in the administrative structure. Regarding political commands, the sanction must also be political, which includes juridical elements and possibly force. Again, sanctions must usually be legitimated and justified, in general as well as in specific terms.

So then, A politically commands and B must obey. B is thus politically subordinate to A. We are therefore speaking of a *vertical* sort of relationship, one which may be more fleeting, somewhat stable or heavily institutionalized (meaning it is and can be regularly repeated and enforced against unwilling subordinates). A's sanctions in relation to B can range from exclusion from positions of power to violent reprisal. Mostly, however, command has a productive rather than sanctioning function and is dynamic. A can create and get things done by means of commands directed to B, C, D, and so on, which A is able to enforce. Yet this is no free position between two equally placed agents. Horizontal positions imply equality, hierarchical positions, inequality. In economic terms it is material inequality, bureaucratically it is administrative inequality, politically it is inequality regarding relations within the political dimension specifically – that is, in what regards the definitions of whatever goals are to be achieved politically in any collective endeavour in societies in which the political dimension has been established. In other words, this inequality not only relates to the *means* (which is typical of bureaucratic hierarchies), but especially to the *ends*. Thus far, I have basically referred to commands of A over B as though we were speaking exclusively of individuals. This is indeed the most elementary relationship we can pinpoint in any social formation. However, command – like the other possible universal types of coordination of social relations in human societies – also connects A and B as collectivities placed in vertical, hierarchical relations. Somehow political commands must be deemed legitimate insofar as those above are supposed to be entitled to rule, their actions often being purportedly concerned with and directed to the good of the society they politically rule.

This definition of 'command' is of an analytical character. In real life, it is usually found in combination with 'market' and 'network' 'principles of organization', which have, respectively, 'voluntary exchange' and 'voluntary collaboration' as their 'mechanisms of coordination'. Command implies no voluntary acquiescence, even when the one being commanded would not necessarily be willing to disagree and/or not comply, even rather the opposite. The point is that A *could* force B to comply. Command is the mechanism of coordination of hierarchical relationships, resting on differences of power between agents. These are the three sorts of elementary relations that underpin the whole of social life (Domingues 2017/2018, ch. 7). With command, therefore, we take the first, but decisive, step towards penetrating the whole of authoritarian collectivism as it is structured in the political dimension. Let us start to unpack what this means.

In authoritarian collectivism, political commands are linked to hierarchical political relations. They are vertical and pervasive. Those who do not obey can be sanctioned according to the decisions of those in superordinate positions. This is no symmetrical relation. Political commands imply political goals – ends, not merely means. They are, therefore, not put forward by the bureaucracy. Having said that, the bureaucracy as such may be a part of the political system. This includes the top layers of the armed forces, which were, incidentally, often decisive for the victory of twentieth-century 'socialism' (through national liberation and popular wars, guerrillas and the like). To be sure, we are proposing an analytical perspective of the subject here, one which may, in real life, be less clear-cut than what we can define conceptually. Yet the political dimension can be found in modern political systems too, while authoritarian collectivism is a sort of postmodern social formation. Political systems in modernity are based to a large extent on political command – whatever their characteristics and whatever the political regimes that steer them (democracy, fascism, bureaucratic authoritarianism, Bonapartism). Political command can be 'paternalistic' and well meant, stirring up enthusiasm and mobilization, yet it remains vertical, especially if it is exercised to the detriment of real participation (Cuban 'socialism', despite all its luminosity and hopefulness, has always evinced this shortcoming, as even sympathetic observers perceived – Huberman and Sweezy 1969, ch. 11).

Horizontal political relations are also present in modernity, depending on the equality (real or imagined) between citizens. Here, of course, the market plays a role too, in that one can buy political compliance, either through the use of money or some other sort of barter. The same is true of authoritarian collectivism, but command played a stronger role in these postmodern societies than it does even in modern ones. In authoritarian collectivism most political relations, from fleeting interactions to deeply institutionalized relationships, were premised on hierarchical political command, though the market mechanism, via some sort of barter, might be present. Horizontal networks were usually not accepted, except to some extent within closed organizational settings (e.g. party cells, oligarchic collective political directions).

An additional feature of this sort of society is that the division between public and private was extremely restricted. It did not disappear entirely, but any domain was within the reach of state commands. Of course, the economy – in contradistinction to capitalism – was placed within the state domain, either directly or indirectly (as often with collectivized peasant property), and 'planning' was subsumed under the 'command economy'. 'Needs', starting with what should be produced and consumed, came under party command. But all spheres of life were so defined, except as regards personal property and individual life, even if in this case things were not absolute. They were all subjected, at least potentially, to state command, although to some extent 'socialist legality' stabilized the expectations of citizens in this regard. Once this was established, the citizenry knew what state interference they could expect in various domains of social life. Such interference was broader and more intense or more limited and milder in different countries and in different periods.

We shall touch on command and the state below, beyond the political dimension proper. Let us now examine how political commands operate more specifically in authoritarian collectivism.

Chapter 3

THE PARTY-STATE AND POLITICAL COMMANDS

Commands – that is, *political commands* – in this sort of twentieth-century social formation were issued fundamentally by what has been called the *party-state*, of which the first element – the party – was actually the defining one (Kornai 1992, 34–41).[1] The state was larger and comprised many other components and processes. The political component was always linked directly to the party, although bureaucratic elements could be articulated with it. Hence, the formal frontiers between the party and state/society in general did not correspond exactly to what was legally formalized. The same can be said of families, in principle not directly connected to politics or the party, whose influence as a part of party relations could be very strong.

This was the core of a historically specific system of rule. What really matters here is how vertical, hierarchical and based on command the system came to be. This was neither what the Bolsheviks had envisaged nor what they had originally practised (an issue to which I will return below). Yet once the Soviet state was consolidated, the soviets – which had been the focus of the revolutionary process – were entirely subordinated to the party, which controlled all the state bureaucratic machinery. Whether staffed by former Czarist functionaries or by new party cadres, the system came to rest absolutely on hierarchical relations, namely command and compliance. In the newly established imaginary this was related to two ideas: the 'dictatorship of the proletariat' and 'democratic centralism'.

Vladimir Ilyich Ulianov, or simply Lenin ([1917] 1964), discussed the 'dictatorship of the proletariat' in his *The State and Revolution*, which he ended, however, without examining the development of Soviet power and its prospects. While the bourgeois state was based on bourgeois class power and consisted in an instrument of exploitation for that ruling class, Lenin envisaged the proletarian state – the 'dictatorship if the proletariat' – as a state that would develop towards its own disappearance, its 'withering away'. It would be so simple that even a 'cook' could manage it, which meant that bureaucracy could and would disappear too. Marx's ([1871] 1986) analysis of the Paris Commune – which was in fact influenced above all by anarchists – furnished the main foundations for Lenin's view of the future, the construction of socialism and the eventual emergence of communism, as well as that of the proletarian state and its disappearance. Before this happened, however, the bourgeois state had to be 'smashed'. Lenin was, moreover, very much concerned with the necessity of keeping power at all costs – the fragility of the Commune and the massacre of the communards had not vanished from the memory of the revolutionaries (Badiou 2009). The well-known anecdote that Lenin danced on the snow the day after Soviet power outlived the Commune expresses this poignantly. And he did what was needed to be done to keep power, ruthlessly when push came to shove (though comparing Bolshevik repression to Stalin's terror is simply non-sensical), while expecting a revolution in Europe that never came to rescue the embattled Soviet Russia, eventually the Soviet Union, and its breakthrough. Lenin was, however, incapable of theorizing this stalemate – which implied an extremely high cost, for himself and socialism – either in the last pages of his main book on the state or afterwards.

Curiously, despite their acidic critique of liberalism, Marx ([1871] 1986) and Lenin ([1917] 1964) to some extent took up one key aspect of its original outlook. In the 'dictatorship of the proletariat', the eternal squabble of parliamentarianism would disappear and communism would eventually get rid of politics. As Engels ([1878] 1975, 262), inspired by Saint-Simon ([1820] 1967, 181) and later resumed by Lenin, noted, the 'rule over men' would give way to the 'administration of things' and the 'direction of production'.[2] Then 'the state dies out' (*stirbt ab* or 'withers away', as the phrase is often translated into English). This was a reproduction of liberalism's first incarnation, though originally the idea was expressed juridically rather than technically: the social pact that created the state aimed at simply impeding any harm being done against the pristine rights of individual citizens. The state was, therefore, in principle very passive. This did not last long since the emergence of social issues and questions with different sources forced liberalism to change and accept the political dynamic that the political dimension of modernity had introduced, with the state becoming active and aiming at the future. In a strange turn of events, Marxists kept the former outlook of liberalism in what regards the complete development of the new civilization they strived for. If in the short or medium run class struggle implied politics, the latter would eventually disappear once classes vanished. In fact, power would no longer exist as such: absolute freedom would come about, whatever this was supposed to mean, and only 'things' would be commanded. Although this whole process would take time to unfold, prior to that even under socialism and proletarian rule parliamentarianism would be superseded by the practical workings of sound working class committees.

Needless to say, this was a vacuous projection. Power was as important as ever, and the emerging new social formation took over politics from modernity, made it absolute and superimposed it upon all other dimensions of social life. The state was never even close to 'dying out', rather the opposite: it expanded to encompass nearly all spheres of life. On the other hand, administrative techniques were formally stripped of their political underpinnings and taken as neutral even in what regards class struggle (especially in the economy), as if their genesis did not, perhaps indelibly, stamp their existence.

The second issue – 'democratic centralism' – was forced by Lenin ([1921] 1965) on the party in the early 1920s, in the midst of fierce internal disagreements and struggles, as well as the counter-revolutionary menace. Whether this was in turn 'forced' on him by reality – that is, the fear of collapse and defeat – or corresponded to his original views of the party, which for their part had been, in the beginning of the century, the object of vicious polemics, is basically impossible to determine. Simply calling him a Jacobin dictator, though, helps little in the understanding we could develop of the question.[3] In any case, the faith in the identity between party, state and class, as well as in the simple 'nationalization' of production, opened the gateway to the destruction of democracy without many misgivings, once it was supposedly guaranteed that eventually things would self-correct, a faith which was not actually spelt out. The growing authoritarianism was strengthened by Joseph Stalin's ([1930] 1955) truly far-reaching innovation according to which, paradoxically but arguably dialectically, the state should become *stronger* in socialism before it 'withered away'. Stalin's state was fundamentally an instrument of the party, which was, ultimately, an instrument of its ruling circle that would rule with absolute recourse to that at least in part ad hoc mechanism introduced by Lenin. Curiously, and sadly in fact, 'democratic centralism' was perhaps the only true political invention of the twentieth century (Walles 1981). It proved to be a very authoritarian one, despite the promise dubiously contained in its explicit phrasing.

The 'dictatorship of the proletariat' as such implied that command, especially political command, over the former ruling classes was warranted and necessary, at a collective level. This also found expression in the command exercised over specific groups and individuals – such as the so-called 'kulaks', 'saboteurs', 'wreckers', remaining bourgeois individuals, and so on depending on the time and the wins of the party and of the party's direction or autocrat. Potential or actual repression always accompanied the commands the party issued, even when there was compliance with general as well as specific commands, should other political imperatives arise. Afterwards, even when repression subsided and new terms were used to name 'socialist' states, such as 'all-people's state' or 'popular democracies', the mechanisms of command

and repression remained, of course, in place. 'Democratic centralism', which terminated the existence of 'factions' within the Bolshevik party, was a complement to that broader structure. In principle, democracy was putatively the key element: discussion should be open and free, participatory. Once a decision was reached, however, the centre of the party – the central committee and the political bureau – would, along with the organization's full membership, simply implement the democratically taken decisions. That is, horizontality should be the paramount way to proceed, with the voluntary collaboration of party members. From this, it was transplanted to the state: not only party members, but also the working class and, furthermore, the whole population would be involved in the dynamic of democratic centralism. This was, however, simply not true in the end: verticality and hierarchy carried the day, and authoritarianism prevailed.

The notion of 'democratic centralism' was then exported to the whole world and also applied where there was no 'dictatorship of the proletariat', but rather 'popular democracy' or similar and looser formulations, according to which broader class alliances were in place. In any case, we would find it in Eastern Europe and, overall, in the Balkans as well as in China, Vietnam, Laos, Cambodia, Cuba and some African countries, but also in Yugoslavia, regardless of its partial 'self-management' schemes in industry, which were an exception within authoritarian collectivism (Djilas 1957; Kornai 1992). Since it was political hierarchies that really mattered, simple variations vis-à-vis administration were basically inconsequential in this respect (with some of them remaining – North Korea – or becoming even more brutally repressive – Romania and Albania – as their situation soured).

In practice, democratic centralism became a very shallow ideological cover for the centralization of all decisions within the party and, further, its top decision-making centres, whenever such decisions were – in general or in specific terms – important enough to merit their attention, whether it was a new electoral law, a five-year plan or related to a prominent dissident. Command by the party-state and particularly its main decision-making centres lied at the core of authoritarian collectivism, Kuron and Modzelewski's aforementioned idea of a 'central political bureaucracy' as a ruling collectivity therefore being fully warranted. This was facilitated by the disappearance of private property, with the 'nationalization' of all the means of production and the centralization of property being placed in the hands of the state. Given the blueprint of the *The Communist Manifesto* (Marx and Engels [1848] 1978), this was the strategic step for the construction of socialism and a common tenet of all socialists and communists during the twentieth century. Leon Trotsky ([1935] 1956, [1938a] 1977) himself almost to the end believed that he could define the Soviet Union as a 'degenerate workers' state' because state property remained, despite the political regime being usurped by the Thermidorian bureaucracy. Eventually, however, he had to admit, even if hesitantly, that something new had actually emerged which was not socialism, though the working class had not yet said, he believed, the 'last word' (Trotsky [1937] 2004, 80, 180–88).

The puzzle was overwhelming: if the collectivization of property per se did not entail the state taking on a workers' character, what would? Hegedus (1976, 22–23) realized that the 'lawful' owner – the state itself – could not exercise its 'property rights' directly, though he was not troubled by this. Professionals, who became independent of society, something not necessarily negative, were in charge. In fact, however, only a very dogmatic and economistic perspective could underlie such a poor statist definition of socialism. Korsch ([1919] 1969, 30, 34ff.) underlined this early on. In the end, the authoritarianism of the party-state and the structure of command it entailed, in which popular power played hardly any role, precluded the flourishing of socialism, even if we accept – which is not really so simple a point – that the collectivization of the means of production via state monopoly is tantamount to the construction of the basis of socialism.

The bureaucracy was indeed a key element in the structuration of authoritarian collectivism. As noted above, the armed forces, emerging as large bodies after revolutionary armed struggles, guerrilla or otherwise, were usually crucially important in this, although with varying degrees of hidden decisiveness (more in China, Cuba, Vietnam and Angola than even the Soviet Union, let alone Czechoslovakia, Poland and East Germany). Bureaucracy, in its several branches, worked mostly through the mechanism of command, in order to make good the hierarchical presuppositions on which it rested, as in fact it always does wherever it mushrooms. And it mushroomed everywhere – in collectivist as well as in capitalist countries. Yet it implied command in relation to means, not to ends. It is important to remember that ends can be means and means ends in the 'muddling through' of administration, especially if the bureaucracy is a low-skilled and incompetent one, never listens to citizens and moves in a ritualistic and stupid manner, or when it is intent on bending or creating devious new rules and norms.

Leaders of communist parties in all such countries usually loathed bureaucracy. They intensely criticized it. They were at the least wary of it. In fact, bureaucracy did create many problems and bottlenecks, irritating also the population. Mao Zedong in particular hated it and was aware of the dangers of 'vested interests' for socialism, though he stopped short of naming the latter (Mao [1967] 1977, 21). But this means nothing for the definition of the system of authoritarian collectivism. The bureaucracy did not rule, the party did, and within the party, the higher one went the more powerful cadres were. They were the ones who exercised political command and set the goals, regardless of how much these might mutate into means, conversely, and means into ends in their bureaucratic implementation. Administrative command is, nevertheless, what really defines bureaucratic hierarchies, in contradistinction to hierarchical party political command.

Consequentialism – that is, the idea that means are subordinate to ends and that the latter justify the former, whatever these might be – was deeply ingrained in this way of thinking. This lies at the core of Stalinism, was present in Leninism, but found a more explicit formulation in Trotsky ([1938b] 1973). In these extreme forms, consequentialism was decisive for the tragedy of twentieth-century communism, with constant transgression of ethical limits and also as a disguise for emerging forms of political inequality and domination. Political command, when revolutionaries were in power, was cut across by such political imperatives and consequentialism, and the struggle for power much too often came to be strongly marked by this sort of perspective as well. The brightness of and certainty about the future buttressed it (though one cannot really say that this was true of Marx, their foremost theoretical reference, since he held a more Hegelian outlook that was neither a utilitarian nor a Kantian absolute sort of morality).

Bureaucracy was important for the structuration of the party, and it developed its own specific machinery. It often had political responsibilities and several bureaucrats became important political cadres, especially during the last phase of the Soviet Union and today in China's reformulated social formation (even though they tend to become more technocratic as countries develop). Bureaucrats at all levels and later on these more sophisticated 'technocrats' had considerable political clout and power, even when they were not party members but were well networked with party instances at the level they worked (though to ascend to all important positions usually demanded party membership). They could then exercise political command, not merely administrative command. This achieved its pinnacle with the planned economy – or 'command economy', as it should more properly be denominated (Nolan 1995, 3–7). This economy, despite consisting in a complicated bargaining process and resulting in a large amount of waste, appeared – or was presented – to society at large as the distillation of rationality, with command over 'needs' as well, bizarrely leading to permanent scarcity (Fehér, Heller and Márkus 1983, 77ff.; Lin 2006).

At this stage, it is important to recall a crucial issue, namely, that modernity created for the first time – and perhaps the only time – the political dimension, including specific institutions and an important swath of the modern imaginary. Politics, in terms of state and society, therefore arose with the establishment of the political dimension, with its special, open features. It was partly detached from morals and initially neutralized in what concerns explicit power and conflicts, which multiplied immediately. Political command, network and market-coordinating mechanisms were part and parcel of such developments, being as they were connected to decision making and the definition of ends. If the state was not alone in the structuration of political modernity, it was at least the central actor herein. The bureaucracy modern states – and business firms – counted on was also very specific, of a non-patrimonial kind, regardless of deviations (ever since regarded as criminal). Administrative command as well as network collaboration (usually against formal rules) and different sorts of voluntary market-oriented bargains and exchanges were also part and parcel of its constitution.

Authoritarian collectivism embraced them both, that is, political and bureaucratic command, centred on the party-state and its upper decision-making echelons, but in practice tried to get rid of or at least to downplay those other mechanisms, with detrimental consequences, later reforms introduced to minimize the latter usually failing (see Nove [1983] 1999). It is worth remembering that socialism was supposed to promote the network principle of organization, whence voluntary collaboration would spread across the world and eventually arrive at a purer form of 'association of free persons' – that is, communism (Marx [1867] 1962, 92). This would happen initially through the development of full democracy, eventually through a sort of spontaneous coordination of all social agents, though how exactly this would come about was never really detailed.

Since Marx ([1843a] 1956, 233–50), but especially with Weber ([1921–22] 1980, part II, ch. 6), abstract universalism has been seen as a key component of the imaginary and institutional underpinning of the modern state – as much as of citizenship (Domingues 2019a, chs 1–2). Both Marx and Weber stressed how important this was for the constitution of bureaucracy. Additionally, Marx pointed to the identification of the bureaucrat with the state, even calling it its 'spirit', as well as to the meanness of his career attachments, while Weber conceptualized the fundaments of modern, non-patrimonial and legal–rational bureaucracy, producing what became a well-established, indeed a classical approach in sociology. Even in terms of command, universalism and abstraction play a decisive role. Bureaucrats were, moreover, separated from the means of production and had to strictly abide by the law. The appropriation of state resources – actually society's resources, extracted from it via taxes – is forbidden, and the official who disrespects this may incur severe penalties if uncovered. This characterizes what has been defined in modernity as 'corruption'.

Legal rules thus specify which commands can be given. These tend to be in principle and universally legally framed, although even liberalism or republicanism always recognized legislation with more particularized targets and objectives. The chain of bureaucratic command is also legally formally defined, and what can be done within the state apparatus as well as in its intervention in society falls under the same rules. To be sure, also administratively there have always been regulations that imply, internally or externally, more particularized and even ad hoc commands, which are then, especially as the state grows and assumes several tasks vis-à-vis social life, addressed to different societal collectivities. Yet by and large, in modern states, more particularized commands must be derived from political power, either through legislative or (increasingly) executive power, which are then implemented administratively.

This applied in authoritarian collectivism too. Since the establishment of Soviet power and especially after 'socialist legality' became a key issue in discourse and generally in practice, the bureaucracy was supposed to follow the political commands of the party. Nevertheless, even if these were often universal in scope, application and addressees, many of them were of a particular nature. The bureaucracy was in Soviet-like societies, therefore, entrusted with supposedly rational decisions and had to deal with citizens in particular in a universalist way and treat them abstractly, while keeping their hands off state property and resources. This is true beyond the exceptions of 'bourgeois' and 'anti-social' elements – from the beginning to very late in the development of these societies – though there were many other targets as well.

There were, of course, many systems of favours and informal exchange between citizens and the bureaucracies, particularly among the latter, with little 'formal rationality' in this regard, especially due to arbitrariness and scarcity (Fehér, Heller and Márkus 1983, 106–07, 176 – though these authors exaggerate the lack of general rationality and efficiency of the system, which was able to combine formal and substantive rationality).[4] Initially, voting rights were withheld from bourgeois elements. Later, social rights were not uniformly distributed, with the working class usually being privileged in relation to peasants, to start with in the 1936 Soviet Constitution, though this was, formally at least, later on superseded. The same applies to schemes around the Chinese danwei (the work unit), whose workers were granted entitlements and the famous 'iron rice bowl', whereas peasants were supposed to take care of themselves. Internal passports were introduced in order to control migration to cities (a feature whose stronger survivor is the hukou system of registration in China, exposing migrants to industrializing cities to radical precarity). In practice, the best 'treat' was reserved for the upper layers of these societies, despite relatively modest income differentials (see below), but this does not change the main point here. Overall as well as more specifically, since the party was omnipresent in social life and political commands emanated from it, particularism and an enfeeblement of abstractness and universalism could easily occur. It was enough that some authority, somewhere, so decided. Reification – with a high level of passivity – connected to the definition of citizens in abstract terms did not disappear, yet it was overrun and demoralized by naked human behaviour based on political will and power stemming from particular and particularized sources. This was a dreadful combination.

In this respect, authoritarian collectivism left modernity behind (only to crash into it dramatically or rather smoothly embrace it some decades later), but it still took over many of its elements, some of which were precisely those that the projects of socialism, Marxist or otherwise, were keen to shed in a truly free civilization, as well as developed others that run quite contrary to its emancipatory perspectives. Failing to even approach what its inspirational tenets implied, authoritarian collectivism in the end showed itself largely parasitical of modernity, with bizarre 'deviations' – which were, however, part and parcel of its real functioning – that did not eliminate the abstract reification of state-bureaucratic power but made the arbitrariness of political power much more visible, along with heightened mechanisms of surveillance and repression, as we once again see in the case of contemporary China. This was probably fatal for these societies in the long run, though reconnecting with capitalism did mean that the political apparatus gave itself a new lease of life. I shall return to this below. If other elements were in fact present in its imaginary, which might – though they eventually proved too weak – energize it in a different direction (as Marcuse 1958, 10–11, 265–67, hoped, in his immanent critique of Soviet Marxism), it was the more authoritarian ones that prevailed.

Chapter 4

THE LAW, RIGHTS AND
THE JUDICIARY

As with all such events, the Bolshevik Revolution was messy. It counted on huge popular participation and disruption in the main industrial cities of the empire and jacqueries in the countryside. Other revolutions unfolded over time – such as in China and Vietnam – in the sense that they emerged victorious from a protracted process of warfare, during which major institutions were forged. Others took some time to even start to think about how they would reorganize the state on a permanent basis – this was the case of Cuba. Law, as part of the 'bourgeois state', was not really favoured by Marxist revolutionaries (nor by anarchists, for that matter, though social democrats became very fond of it). First, law was to be exercised by popular courts and the like. Eventually, in the period of 'real socialism' and even more so today, in post-postmodern states, the bureaucracy and the legal professions that were to be discarded by socialism and communism made a comeback. As is well known, the judiciary is a part of the bureaucratic apparatus of the state, although, like the army in this regard, a very specialized part of it (though both, especially the latter, can and have, in authoritarian collectivism as much as in liberal states, taken up political roles at several moments and in different areas). In this, too, authoritarian collectivism ended up replicating some basic features of 'capitalist states', once it left behind the messy period of popular courts and judgements (Grzybowski 1962; Hazard 1969). Yet some crucial changes took place too, at least in what regards the imaginary, and not for the better. This leads us directly towards a discussion of the role of rights in authoritarian collectivism.

Initially, the Russian Revolution had a very indirect approach to rights, speaking of the rights of workers but never taking them as natural rights or rights that accrue universally to individuals qua individuals. That being said, the constitutional development of the Soviet Union was part of what may be termed social constitutionalism since the very beginning. Its main jurists in the 1910s–20s, above all Piet I. Stuchka and Eugeny Pashukanis, despite divergent understandings of law, believed it would disappear in the process of constructing socialism, withering away along with capitalism and, above all, the state. Though sustaining rather different views, both saw communism as what we can define as extended networks, so collaborative that they could be free of law and command.[1] Stuchka was more relevant politically; he even wrote, with Lenin, the first decrees of Soviet power, and became a people's commissary. But it was Pashukanis who became more famous as a theoretician. In any case, both occupied top positions in the Soviet institutes for the study of law.

As the outstanding Soviet jurist at the time, Stuchka ([1921] 1988) tried to produce an original Marxist theory of law. Drawing upon Marx's 'Preface' to *Contribution to the Critique of Political Economy* and *Capital*, he defined law as a 'system of social relations' corresponding to the interests of the ruling class, usually connected to 'organized power', meaning basically the state. It is only in class societies that it exists, with the role of safeguarding private property, which lies at its basis. Three 'juridical forms' characterize law. The first is concrete – a 'living', particularly fundamental one (a formulation in which the influence of Ehrlich's theories about *lebendes Recht* – 'living law' – appears to be strong, though unacknowledged). The other two are abstract. These forms correspond, respectively, (1) directly to the relations of production (hence, to the economic 'infrastructure'), (2) to their formalization and (3) to ideological elaboration (that is to say, to the 'superstructure'). With the 1917 Revolution a new system of law was born, Stuchka claimed, which was simplified and based on workers' power. He wanted to rid Marxist theory of the 'will' perspective, stressing the objective content of law and class interests as its underpinnings (Stuchka [1919] 1988, 28; [1921] 1988). Before bourgeois state law, there had been feudal law; after bourgeois law, proletarian law would be, as he had already formerly defined it, the law of the 'transitional period' towards communism, where it would then disappear (Stuchka [1919] 1988; also [1925-27] 1988). Citizenship and rights, for their part, curiously feature in his argument only when he discusses bourgeois law, not in socialism.

In his truly famous and ingenious, though also reductive, *Law and Marxism: A General Theory*, Pashukanis ([1924] 2017) tried to reproduce Marx's analytical approach. If the commodity was the 'cell-form' of capitalist relations in *Capital*, the 'juridical subject' – abstract – was the 'commodity owner' himself, and the basic 'juridical cell' (the main juridical 'form') was the *contract*, between private, atomized agents, separated from their membership in the political society. A 'juridical fetishism' was thus superimposed on the 'fetishism of the commodity'. Private law – arising from economic relations – furnished the basis upon which public law was built and a specific, specialized caste took charge of both. Citizenship and rights did not play any significant role in Pashukanis' argument, although he recognized the relevance of the principles of liberty and equality, as well as that the relations he analyzed lay at the root of natural rights theories. More importantly, once property disappeared and the state, its coercive guarantor along with it, law would no longer exist. While 'revolutionary legality' was not to be denied under the dictatorship of the proletariat, which acted according to the 'conscious will' of the new ruling class, in a period in which private property, law and the state were becoming, in tandem, less significant until the state eventually 'withered away' (Pashukanis [1927] 1980).[2] Even very directly in the sphere of law – almost without mediation – the economy would have the upper hand, since private law, through the contract, would take precedence, in capitalism, over the state and public law, a very arguable and – as Stuchka for one noted – mistaken thesis.

Stuchka was very important, from his senior political position, in propelling Pashukanis's career, with strong praise of his book. But he also criticized him for not paying closer attention to the link between law and state power, which was indeed *class power* (Stuchka [1924] 1988, 11; [1925–27] 1988, 146). Pashukanis ([1927] 1980, [1932] 1980) accepted the criticism as to that specific point but denied the accusation of 'economism' directed at his theory, charging Stuchka instead with reducing law to the relations of production, a point which was well taken but which should have been directed against his own theory, too. The liveliness of this debate, which engaged other jurists too, was, however, not to last. Regardless of how we access and evaluate Stuchka's and Pashukanis's theories, their insights were sophisticated and pointed in several interesting directions, but they were lost in the Soviet Union afterwards. With Stuchka already dead, after a great deal of harassment, eventually, under pressure from the menacing development of Stalinism, Pashukanis ([1936] 1980) produced a stark self-criticism: he had been, he purportedly avowed, formerly disarmed in the face of the 'class enemies'. In socialism the state must grow, he belatedly pretended to recognize, trying to appease Stalin, to no avail. This was not enough to save his prestige, his position or even his life.

If the 1924 Constitution, the first of the Soviet Union, was a sketchy document, in 1936 it adopted a full charter – the so-called 'Stalin Constitution'. By then Stuchka and Pashukanis were disgraced and dead, and the debate was closed. Stalin's close collaborator, former Menshevik and a leading Moscow prosecutor, Andrey Vyshinsky (1948) became the new star of Russian jurisprudence, smearing the memory of both those pioneering jurists and others who collaborated with them. Since there would be no withering away of the state for a long time, law and a constitutional framework were therefore necessary, though shortly after the promulgation of the document that was supposed to strengthen 'socialist legality', the Soviet Union was ravaged by the most notorious and numerous deeds known as 'Stalin's crimes'.[3] State command was at the core of the new legal lore. As it was formerly, too, the dictatorship of the proletariat was paramount, while Soviet democracy was formally reaffirmed. Moreover, law was now firmly placed at the superstructure, though it also corresponded to a specific level of development of the productive forces, such as grasped and formalized by the party, leading some to speak of a Marxist view of 'natural law' (Brunner 1966; 1970).

Vyshinsky was an ally – an accomplice, in fact – of Stalin, but it must be recognized that his solution for socialist law was not absurd, though it was very authoritarian even in the way it was phrased. Since it was clear that the state – and law, consequently – would not wither away any time soon, the country needed a legal framework which should stabilize it, though the party and initially especially Stalin, the autocrat, never accepted the limitations it imposed. While the theory of the state in the Soviet Union and by and large in the 'socialist' world was eventually crystalized as a homage to Lenin's *The State and Revolution* and remained, in principle, the valid understanding of the dictatorship of the proletariat as well as of socialism and communism, Stalin's view in practice totally dislodged that semi-anarchist perspective. In law nothing similar existed. This left a void in which a dispute was staged and easily won by the Stalin–Vyshinsky duo when the former consolidated his power and needed, in order to buttress a strong and durable state apparatus, a more traditional understanding of law. This lent the state and the party the means to rule, and a view of rights close to positivism, implying their absolute objectivity and at best a derived and secondary subjective aspect.

On paper, the 1936 Constitution – and those that followed it decades later – returned to a stronger form of social constitutionalism, formally closer to liberalism, but incorporating elements probably derived from the 1918 Weimar Constitution, with its famous social section and path-breaking 'fundamental rights' (*Grundrechte*), including social rights in the concept of 'material' or 'substantive' rights. Fundamental rights replaced a priori natural rights (see Neumann, [1930] 1978). The one responsible for this link was probably Karl Radek, the Polish-German-Russian cadre, who was originally a member of Lenin's personal circle, an important figure in the Third International, liaison with the German communists and responsible for the study of foreign constitutions in the committee that prepared the 1936 Soviet constitutional draft (as well as once disgraced, rehabilitated, then disgraced again and prosecuted, eventually jailed by Stalin and killed while in prison, in all likelihood upon orders of the latter). Radek was surely aware of the German debates as well as of other constitutional documents, such as the 1917 Mexican Constitution, the first social constitutional document in history. Yet the subjective aspect was entirely subordinate to the state 'will', as the representative of the will of the proletariat, and its objectification, whereby the state, led by the Communist Party, 'granted' rights and freedoms to the 'toilers' (Vyshinsky 1948, 627). Moreover, in daily practice the party held discretion and could interfere with the workings of the law, if necessary due to state instrumental reasons, though of course this was never fully stated (as 'reason of state' teachings, of course, always stress).

The Soviets deemed the 1936 Constitution 'the most democratic constitution in the world'. At the same time, the worst violence and illegality in the history of the Soviet Union were unleashed just after its promulgation, starting with the infamous Moscow Trials.

The Constitution evinced a nice framework, featuring many rights, which privileged urban workers but did not formally pit them against peasants. It was exported everywhere as a model for whatever socialist constitution was adopted in any country. It was moulded after Western constitutions, and it had an especially strong positivist background (thus at variance with the Weimar document), cast according to the tradition of continental 'civil law' (versus Anglo-American 'common law'), though Western jurists were never quoted by Vyshinsky, save for, as usual, in very negative and abusive terms (Grzybowski 1962). Eventually, this juridical mould gave rise to its own distinctive legal 'family', to make use of the language of comparatists (Merryman [1977] 1985, 1–4).

What is particularly relevant, to begin with, is the position of rights in this respect. In Western juridical thought, it once played – and has been playing again – a central role. Indeed, liberalism attributed a paramount position to rights, since the social pact and ensuing constitutions were crafted in order to defend those rights, initially contemplated in the mould of natural rights doctrines and playing a profoundly revolutionary role against the power of the state – first that of the absolutist state, then that of the very modern liberal state. However, rising in Britain already in the early hours of the French Revolution and affirming the power of the state against the universality and priority of rights, positivism challenged this view head on. Austin and especially Bentham were absolutely fundamental to this, the latter notoriously speaking of human rights as 'non-sense upon stilts'. Rights were in their view not universal; they were merely instrumentally attributed to individuals by the state, according to utilitarian considerations. Implicitly, they could be withdrawn if the state thought it necessary. Even in Kelsen and then other positivists we find this inversion (Domingues 2019a, chs 1–3).

Post-revolutionary 'real socialist' jurisprudence adopted the same language vis-à-vis rights. But the way it did this brought it close to positivism. If initially especially Stuchka, who was very close to Lenin, rejected the universality of individual rights and substituted it with the role of social classes, the Stalin Constitution and the legal reasoning accompanying it took a direction similar to that which we find in Bentham's teachings. Rights were, consequently, something the Soviet state granted its citizens according to possibility and opportunity. In spite of this, Vyshinsky was adamant on the far more advanced character of rights and law in the Soviet Union, as compared to capitalist nations as well as regarding its radically more democratic character. This limitation of rights was true despite – or precisely because of, he would actually argue – the leading role it reserved for the Communist Party. Even if it is certainly the case that the Weimar Constitution included a view of 'fundamental rights' and that it did influence the Soviet 1936 Constitution, this in any case did not change the instrumental view of rights as established by the state and the party. Nor does it seem warranted to speak of a 'natural rights' perspective (even if we take them as 'objective') due to the underlying importance of the development of productive forces and its impact on the superstructure, though this became stronger after Stalin's and Vyshinsky's deaths (Brunner 1966; 1970).

In a liberal constitutional framework and the imaginary of modern societies, rights have priority, at least formally, despite the strong influence of positivism. In principle the state cannot tamper with them, although social rights and social policy, with more concrete features, have complicated the equation since they can hardly be seen as given or unchanging. When we examine the Soviet legal framework, we see the opposite, despite the proviso regarding social rights. In the conjunction of the supposed class character of the state and, therefore, of socialist law – even if it eventually belongs to all people and not merely to the working class and the role the state and especially the party are to perform in political and social life – rights become a subordinate element in the general constitutional scheme. Yet the issue is actually broader, since law is not fixed, even constitutionally, but rather exists as a means to steer social life: law in general and rights in particular are means through which the party-state furthers its ends and steers society politically. It changes course and laws, hence also rights, change according to its political designs.

This brings us back to the issue of general commands, abstraction and reification, which characterize bureaucracy as much as law, on the one hand, and the particularized commands, of a political nature, which evince the often-arbitrary exercise of power in a rather naked way. This could not but be detrimental to the legitimation of the system. Parasitical of modernity, since the innovations it introduced in the ambit of universalism were limited, authoritarian collectivism was forced to shed, either in theory or in practice, part of the legal scaffolding upon which much of what had been emancipatory in it depended. Citizens in modernity were, according to natural rights theory and even within positivist currents, to be taken as abstract and thus subjects of abstract universal rights, often framed by so-called 'rigid' constitutions, whether or not this was really respected. This was already discussed by Marx ([1843b]

1956), and Pashukanis tried to find a theoretical solution for it (though his was not really a good one, I believe: see Domingues (2019a, ch. 1) for a discussion of the 'citizenship form', 'rights form' and law in modernity). Pashukanis, as seen above, would jettison the very idea of rights. The 1936 constitutional text, for its part, but especially legal practice, inconsistently mixed those two principles: party-prerogative and citizenship individual rights. This, from the very beginning, affected the legitimation of the system, a problem that became increasingly salient.

In reality, there were no limits to what the state – and above all the party – could do. No private matter was out of their reach, no rights were universally and a priori secured. This buttressed the unfortunate repressive nature of such states to extents that went far beyond anything Marx and Engels (and probably even Lenin) ever imagined and would ever have condoned. On the other hand, since rights did not in principle belong to the individual as such but rather were *granted* by the state, supposedly as a decision of its ruling class (workers alone or workers and peasants) or the whole people, but obviously of a ruling stratum at whose core the Communist Party and its superior decision-making centres lay, such an attribution of rights assumed a rather paternalistic character. This perspective was present everywhere in authoritarian collectivism and was expressed perhaps nowhere more directly than in the German Democratic Republic, where themes were recovered from the Weimar Republic but also especially from Bismarck's period and his pioneering, though restricted, introduction of social rights in a rather paternalistic fashion (Jarausch [1998] 2012).

In authoritarian collectivism, we are hence fundamentally dealing with a 'prerogative state' which adopts, for its interventions in social life, 'rule by law', and not the rule of law, at least when the party so decided. The latter would evince equality regarding the law, predictability and uniformity in its basic framework, including the limitation of state power (Peerenboom 2002). Moreover, the society and state divide was not truly relevant in this kind of state, nor was the private and public divide, even though the state did not actually encompass everything (a small sphere of individual rights was kept, mainly in relation to family and personal property). Law was developed in authoritarian collectivism within this framework, its private dimension being always rather restricted, except to some extent in some Eastern European countries, such as Czechoslovakia (Grzybowski 1962, 144ff.). In Soviet legal structure and thinking, the party was the motor of policy and the bureaucracy its executor. Things could change suddenly; ministries and other organs could shift policy and hence law at any time, bringing considerable uncertainty for social agents legally and politically, though for long stretches of time, once Stalin died and Stalinism in its more radical expression was discarded, some predictability could be found in the application of law and the recognition of individual rights. Law was, therefore, seen not as the basis for horizontal relations between rights-holding citizens but as an element in the hierarchical mechanism of the party-state and the basis for its capacity to issue commands (though certainly many breaches of the so-called 'socialist legality' were typical of political repression, another sort of more direct command).

To be sure, one could claim that law was enacted by democratically elected and managed Soviets. But this was, unfortunately, simply untrue, despite a façade of democracy and legality. I will return to this issue below. In any case, this was the framework that was exported to all the countries that followed the Soviet Union, even when they clashed with it politically, namely China, Czechoslovakia, Vietnam and Cuba (Tapia-Valdés 1977; Yu 1989; Gillespie 2004; Mo 2010; Hualing, Gillespie, Nicholson and Parlett 2018; Bertot Triana 2019).

At the same time, we see a complex evolution of the juridical system. Here, trajectories vary significantly. Many authoritarian collectivist countries already had well-constituted court systems, especially in Eastern Europe, while others did not. Conversely, in Asia in particular other traditions, such as courts and judiciary procedures steered by local gentry, offered distinct patterns of judiciary work. Where change stemmed from revolutions with popular participation, there was also a greater initial change in the judicial system, with popular courts taking over and applying popular notions of justice (and often retribution against local potentates, landlords and suchlike). But overall there was a trend towards professionalization and bureaucratization of courts of law – above all superior courts but not only – although with lay participation remaining a usual feature of many of these systems. Mostly justice without political command was meted out to offenders in a more or less harsh criminal system, with civil codes having their importance radically diminished since property and business disputes were, to start with, rather limited. Labour law also played a lesser role in a system in which workers were supposedly the ultimate collective property holders. Family law, on the other hand, was well developed.

Here, we face a radical form of fetishism – one that plays a crucial role in this sort of social formation, rooted in a Marxist conception that took on, however, a different meaning once it was institutionalized in the Soviet Union and other 'socialist' countries. In modern liberal societies, with their individualistic legal system, it is the abstract relations between individual legal agents that establish the 'form' whereby the experience (*Erlebnis*, in fact) of agents is framed and upon which a whole imaginary universe is built and even the alienation of labour power, hence exploitation, is made possible (Domingues 2019a, ch. 1). In authoritarian collectivism, it is the idea of collective property as state property that plays this role. State property makes the working class and individual workers the formal owners of the means of production and even most of the means of consumption. However, in reality these are appropriated by the core political agents, individual and collective, of the bureaucratic system (Kuron and Modzelewski, [1966] 1982, ch. 1). This entails real relations of domination, political and economic, including exploitation, of a smaller section of society over the majority.

When ordinary legislation and practice happened to stumble on sensitive political matters, things could change drastically and relations of domination would come explicitly to the fore. The party would then step in and make sure its prerogatives were attended to, especially if high functionaries were involved in criminal deeds or if political dissidence and conflict surfaced. In any case, judges belonged to the party and were subordinate to its discipline with, of course, more particularized attention dedicated to them the higher they were placed in the hierarchical ladder. In this regard, once again we see a good deal of continuity with modernity, with a similar judicial system having been built, although often with greater popular participation as well as direct political interference.

A particular feature of authoritarian collectivist judicial systems is the role of the public prosecutor. Prosecutors concentrated three functions in their hands, over and above courts and lawyers: they prosecuted cases, of course, made sure law was applied properly by courts and received citizens' complaints. This, again, shows how command went over and above rights: in authoritarian collectivism, prosecutors were relatively efficient in responding to the grievances expressed by citizens, provided that no sensitive political issues were broached and no top officials were accused.

In China, a particularly interesting development took place within the Yan'an Way, a vast ideological mass movement the Communist Party launched in the early 1940s (Xiaopong 2014). Civil law and professionalized justice were dominant during the drawn-out revolution and afterwards. Its unacknowledged source consisted in the models embraced by the republican Chinese Nationalist Party, the Kuomitang – KMT, borrowed in turn from Germany and Japan. Yet a more popularly based sort of adjudication also arose, in which adjudication was often mixed with mediation and conciliation. Basically, judges were to go to the places – mainly villages in the countryside – where problems presented to them had occurred, collect information, talk to the people and bring them together. Finally, they should try to reach a conclusion that engaged the community. Thereby popular justice in some measure took place, though a professional judge pivoted the process and steered solutions. Even though most verdicts received the community's blessing, they were not necessarily consensual beyond sheer public agreement. This contrasted with traditional Western-style formal judicial practice and harked back, with communist innovations, to the way local imperial gentry formerly managed justice in the countryside and villages.

Nonetheless, this was never the hegemonic feature of Chinese law, which was largely bureaucratized and formalized. Such popularly based, grassroots juridical exercises pointed to the strong anti-bureaucratic strand of the Chinese Revolution and especially Maoism, to things like its 'mass line' in political orientation, which were resumed much more intensely or, in an alternative perspective skewed towards voluntarism, with disastrous consequences, during the Cultural Revolution (Bernal 1981; Dirlik 2005). Eventually, however, although the system of law that emerged within the Yan'an Way remained relevant in the countryside, it was the bureaucratic perspective that came to predominate in Chinese authoritarian collectivism, mainly, but not only, in large urban areas. It has, it is worth remarking, roots among others in the old Confucian–Legalist imperial state tradition, with its sophisticated, if highly ritualized, bureaucracy.

Chapter 5

THE NOMENKLATURA: POLITICAL POWER AND SOCIAL PRIVILEGE

One of the thorniest issues in the debate about 'real socialism' was whether this was a class society. If classes are defined by the idea of private property, this was surely not the case. The state was the formal proprietor of all or most of the means of production, although peasants often had some stake in property relations current in these countries, whether some sort of collectivization had taken place or not (mostly it did). Workers were supposed to be the ruling class in these states, yet, as argued above, this was by no means the case. We thus have to ask what 'property' means beyond juridical definitions, as already suggested in the previous section. While this is not the main aim of this book a basic answer to it must be given in order to understand the role of the political dimension and its hold on the whole authoritarian collectivist social formations.

We can say that 'appropriation' means first of all that someone, individually or collectively, takes real control of something. It implies power over the appropriated *object*, either juridically, as we have known since the Romans with their definition of rights in rem (that is, over things). More concretely, it allows for the manipulation of the thing appropriated – whether we eat it, use it to produce something else, play with it or throw it away. It thus implies the power of command over that which is appropriated. This command may be collectively shared through some sort of networked relationship, and this can be, overall, exclusionary. Part of it can also be placed in a temporary lease to smaller groups of workers or, if of limited size, on a more permanent basis.

In the case in point, as part and parcel of the state, the core elements regarding property/appropriation in the party-state were those who had more direct control and discretionary power over most objects in authoritarian collectivism. But this did not occur through individual and private appropriation. Appropriation was always collective and public (though with a high level of secrecy). No one had a private title to appropriate the means of production. The party-state and especially its upper echelons were the actual proprietors of the means of production in these societies and could appropriate the economic surplus as well as social privileges, though on a much smaller scale than capitalists in their adversarial societies. The contours of ruling and proprietary collectivities were to some extent defined from above, according to a list of positions to be filled (hence the 'nomenklatura', in Soviet jargon), higher salaries and perks (though messier than formally planned). It is useless trying to replicate the capitalist class model in authoritarian collectivism, for the former rested on the formal juridical appropriation of the means of production and a clear-cut division between classes. In authoritarian collectivism, it was hierarchical political relations (stretching into, and mixed with, bureaucratic hierarchies) and the power of command that mattered. Political officials and bureaucrats stood out, but the system more amply included a myriad of functions, especially managers in all areas of economic and social life and the top brass of the military, which often stemmed from a period of armed struggle against oppressive and colonial or quasi-colonial regimes.[1] What legitimized the power of command of the party-state was its self-definition as representatives of the 'general interest' (Fehér, Heller and Márkus 1983, 71–72), be it class- or nation-based.

In contradistinction, there were those who were bereft of hierarchical prerogatives and power. Whether there was more or less freedom granted to the new working class as well as to more or less independent peasants is an open issue. Surely there was only one employer, but once the worst of original accumulation was over, more flexibility, benefits and control of workplaces by workers was purportedly obtained, according to some interpretations (Lebowitz 2012, 90–92, 154), although Rizzi ([1939] 1976) spoke of 'collective slavery', since there was authoritarianism and no labour market, hence no freedom for workers

Early on, Nikolai Bukharin (1925, ch. 8), the young and well-learned Bolshevik leader, recognized that the division between party/leaders and class/bases, the former for him the most advanced part of the latter, could engender, through the division of labour, new classes. Yet in his quite orthodox Marxism, he did not doubt that the development of productive forces and the education of the proletariat would prevent that. It did not. Party fetishism, with its purported absolute knowledge and immediate identification with the proletariat, was crucial in furnishing the underpinnings of a nascent ideology. In the 1920s, the nomenklatura system was already being established.

A concentric, top-down, ramified and entwined structure of inequality characterized authoritarian collectivism. Its verticality and all-encompassing character made the distribution of privileges a matter of degree, owing its existence directly to political power, upon which the subordinate bureaucratic hierarchies all depended. This system regulated all hierarchical positions and access to social benefits, shops, education, etc. (Djilas 1957; Bahro 1977, chs

5–6, 9). The nomenklatura did, however, incorporate many former workers and peasants, or people with this sort of family background, within the new ruling-dominant collectivities (which probably largely explains Stalin's success and even popularity, despite the brutality of his rule). Those external to the system were the working classes of authoritarian collectivism – factory workers or peasants – with a fringe of other small proprietors and/or petty bureaucrats, with variable size and importance in all these societies. The reproduction of this system of unequal relations was in full swing in *all* 'socialist' countries, with parents bequeathing privilege and the easiest paths to hierarchical power to their offspring – while others only occasionally and with much greater effort could open the doors to the upper layers of these societies. There were also middle classes, increasingly professionalized, with tighter, looser or no political connections. The recognition of this sort of social stratification is not a matter of moral condemnation, since class relations lock people in and have a logic of self-reproduction, which however must be brought out.

How to conceptualize class in this regard is hence a complex matter which we cannot pursue here. To be sure, it is not a matter of sheer market relation or, as already stated, private appropriation. This should not lead us, however, to the conclusion that Weber's definition of 'status' (versus 'class' and 'party') is the best way to conceptualize it (contrary to Fehér, Heller and Márkus 1983). Instead, a specific system of class relations which is much more like what Giddens (1985, 13) once defined as that of a *class-divided society*, rather than of a *class society*, structured authoritarian collectivism. Giddens observed in the first case a *division that started from within the emerging state*. This could be configurated in different ways, with basis on 'religion' (actually a fraught category as such whose problems I cannot discuss here), with exclusive access to the 'sacred', or due to the control of military capabilities by certain groups. The case of the Soviet Union and the societies that followed its lead was similar. State control was crucial for the nomenklatura structuration and for the political dimension directly as the element from which it projected itself over the whole of society. Accompanying it was a doctrine with considerable resemblance to 'religious' dogma, usually defined as 'Marxism-Leninism', though it was acclimatized in other settings by means of such accretions as Mao Zedong, Ho Chi Minh or Martí 'thought'. The knowledge it provided, along with the purported representation of popular interests – mostly proletarian or workers' – articulated to it, legitimized and justified the system of rule.

The authoritarianism of the political life in these societies was in this regard inevitable. Without censorship and political repression, it would be impossible to maintain the privileged appropriation of the means of production and the social privileges that surplus production allowed to a more or less broad layer of political officials and bureaucrats, including the branch of specialized managers and more powerful military officers who together ruled these countries. If democratization did occur, it would be very difficult to sustain this differentiated appropriation, which was first of all political, hence fragile, and tended to be dissolved by the access of the population to political power. Privileges would also be much more difficult to reproduce once the political – and secondarily bureaucratic – system of nomenklatura was damaged or brought under real pressure, let alone abolished.

Chapter 6

POLITICAL SYSTEMS AND POLITICAL REGIMES

Political systems in modernity mediate between society and state, with their own double face – societal and state-based – and the centrality and predominance of the latter, while the former may, from time to time, be shut down rather brutally and radically (as in the fascist and the bureaucratic authoritarian regimes), although it operates in a reasonable level of freedom under liberal democracy. In authoritarian collectivism the limitation of the societal political system also obtained, with the private and the open public domains being severely constrained, as already observed. It was through the party that society – mainly the ruling sectors but partly also workers, peasants and petty bureaucrats – found a voice up the ladders of power. The mediation between state and society, which in modernity has been undertaken by the political system, was accomplished in authoritarian collectivism basically via the party apparatus, although other bureaucratic channels could be operative too. Democratic centralism has always been at the service of the core, in party and state, justifying the repression of anyone and anything that might challenge or simply disagree with decisions taken or their concrete application.

To be sure, 'everyday politics' was seemingly crucial (and remains so where political systems from this era are still operative) to convey low-intensity information to party hierarchies. This seems to have often been the case, especially regarding peasants, in the absence of open political systems, of what Kerkvliet (2005, ch. 2) has called the 'power of noncollective action', implying some level of passivity. The crux of the matter here, however, is actually the silent and decentred collective subjectivity of peasants and workers in general, with its steady collective causality over party cadres. It can flame up if grievances go unheeded, even ensuing in rebellions, which have not been uncommon under collective authoritarianism. This sort of everyday politics was and is hardly equivalent to democracy or even democratic centralism, since it is diffuse, non-organized, and is always threatened by party-state repression, although it often impacted the restricted societal political system of collective authoritarianism. This impact was, however, muffled due to party control over all organizations, starting with unions and cultural and artistic associations (peasants have not been allowed to organize autonomously in China). If it could have an impact on party decisions, depending on whether the moment was repressive or some easing of tensions was underway, there was no protection for those who took part in debate, especially if their grievances were in contestation to party decisions and policies.

Publicly divergent standpoints and interests, even within the upper echelons, were difficult to fathom. The more skilled politicians in 'Soviet-type' societies, especially in their post-Stalin phase, were nevertheless those who could read and operate this increasingly more complex web of interests and perspectives, in an also increasingly more professionalized and specialized bureaucracy, capable of decisive input in the decision-making process as well as able to navigate regional diversity and command even popular influence, within predefined limits (Hough 1977, especially 4–10, ch. 1, on the party and even the general secretary increasingly performing as 'brokers'). Political and bureaucratic cliques played these games, partly responding to local feeling and demands. The 'totalitarian' model of interpretation, blocking intellectual access to this possibility – insofar as it was incapable of seeing diversity and political struggle within these countries, which were not simply based on repression – was a real analytical drawback.

The death of Stalin and reforms enacted across socialist countries brought some 'pluralism' (or 'corporatism') to the fore. Then an approach ripened which allowed for a more complex and dynamic picture of these societies, in which social reproduction was achieved by varied means and not only through repression and dogmatism. Even the soviets, which had become mere formalities under Stalin, were partly revived in the aftermath of de-Stalinization. Popular participation could be found in the Soviet Union as well as elsewhere, party-induced and under strict control to be sure, but more active involvement seems not to have been unusual (Hough 1977, ch. 4; Hazard 1980, ch. 3; Bahry and Silver, 1990).

Particularly, China offers a complex mix of both possibilities. It was present in the Chinese Communist Party to some extent, which time and again explored the idea of a 'mass line'. The 1960s Cultural Revolution epitomized this perspective. It counted on Mao's support, supposedly against the bureaucracy (but actually largely against the party's own political apparatus), but he terminated it with recourse to the army when things spiraled out of control and students (the basis of the so-called Red Guards) and other agents became too rowdy, factional and destructive (Bernal 1981; Dirlik 2005; Kraus 2012). Mao also backed a sort of theory of 'continuous' or 'permanent' revolution (not Trotskyist, though) (Schram 1971; Esherick 1979). More generally, he advocated that 'walking on two legs' – cadres/experts and the masses – was necessary for the revolutionary process (Mao [1967] 1977, 107). Vietnam, without relinquishing the basic 'real socialism' model, purportedly demonstrated the more 'dialogical' political system, in which, revolving around passive resistance, the masses had greater influence upon authorities, despite the party's traditional top-down and at some points rather fierce model and strategy (Kerkvliet 2005, 36, passim). Revolutionary Cuba in particular showed great popular enthusiasm, though always centred on Fidel Castro's person and directives. Some sort of 'corporatism', along with controlled mass mobilization and some level of vertical consultation – as well as, more limited, horizontal exchange between the 'Mass Organizations' – may be involved in the internal flexibility of the Cuban political system, allowing for its reproduction with a greater level of legitimacy and adaptation (Kapcia 2021, 3–5, 20ff., 181ff.).

Yet there is no reason to assume that political command as such declined as a key defining aspect of this type of system, nor that democracy thrived, even in a circumscribed sense, as would be the case of liberal democracy – which includes limited democratic and variably oligarchic features, along with private property and deep multidimensional inequalities. Democratic centralism always remained at the core of the system, as it does to this day in the countries where the political system has survived, although of course neither party nor much less its top hierarchs had a total hold over society.

Moreover, elections were surely not free, allowing for real competition, even if in a one-party system.[1] Co-optation was central for all political activities. Especially censorship and repression, led by the political police – a specific and crucial branch of authoritarian collectivist bureaucracy – was crucial in the political system of all these countries. Take the Soviet Union: initially repression and what was called 'Red Terror' appeared in the course of the revolution. This was followed by the brutal civil war, then real terror under Stalinist autocracy. Eventually, a more limited system of control and punishment was established. Yet, all authoritarian collectivist regimes implemented it in one way or another.

The stated rationale of repression was the need to fight against counter-revolution, a point that was not necessarily false, since countless attempts were made in these countries by the internal counter-revolution and foreign powers to cripple, kill and oust these governments and the whole system from power, sometimes targeting specific individuals (the uncountable CIA attempts to assassinate Castro are a case in point). Of course, after 70 years in power, the repressive character of the Soviet Union and its satellites, as well as, to this day, of China, Vietnam, Cuba, Laos and North Korea, increasingly in the case of China and radical in that of Korea, can hardly be attributed to the counter-revolutionary threat. Instead, it is related to the very combination of socially and economically privileged power of the ruling collectivities of authoritarian collectivism and their essentially monopolistic control over political power. It cannot be challenged or modified, for the reasons signalled above, in the direction of democratization. This was the lesson the Chinese learnt from Mikhail Gorbachev's failure (this will be further discussed below).

In addition, drawing upon Marx's ([1871] 1986) aforementioned assessment of the short-lived experience of the Paris Commune, Lenin ([1917] 1964) and the Bolsheviks saw the soviets as a mix of executive, legislative and, although with specialised instances, judicial powers, jettisoning the putatively empty talk of parliamentarian democracy and skewed class justice. In the Soviet Union and other countries to which the model was exported, party political command prevailed in the executive and the legislative, and, when deemed necessary, upon the judiciary. Legislative activity was central in law-making, but other sources of law, such as pronouncements of leaders and administrative directives, were also important (Grzybowski 1962, 66–71).

This is not tantamount to saying that the political regimes, which are the more concrete ways through which political systems are organized and operate, were invariable in authoritarian socialism. They varied in different countries as well as in different moments in each of them. Yet, overall, we can distinguish between a more personally autocratic and a more oligarchized sort of political rule in these systems. The latter sometimes included coy elements of democratic participation, but this was always highly controlled from the top-down, dependent upon party steering and subjected to political limits which could easily lead to repression by the political police (Djilas 1957, 40; Tucker 1963; Cohen 1985, ch. 2; Rigby [1977] 1999). We may name these variants autocratic communism and oligarchic communism, evidently not because anything resembling communism could be found in them, but because the Communist Party was at their very core – even if subordinated to autocrats and oligarchs – and articulated the whole functioning of society. This, however, tends to confuse things insofar as, strictly speaking, these are not forms of communism at all. Another conceptual solution is therefore necessary, starting from the concept of authoritarian collectivism.

Stalin's regime was the ultimate representative of its autocratic regime (though Pol Pot represented an even more violent incarnation of it), which was preceded by and followed by oligarchic regimes, the former already operative in Lenin and Trotsky's time. Autocratic rule can be so brutal that even the party loses any real capacity to exert any influence, becoming a mere instrument of the autocrat. Other possibilities of oligarchy, more conflictual or more harmonic, with important single leaders, could be found, respectively, in China under Mao and Cuba under Castro, including mostly leaders from the 'popular war' and guerrilla periods.[2]

In Cuba, this implied tension and sometimes a conflict between an 'inner circle' of mostly ex-guerrilla members and the cadres of the People's Socialist Party (PSP – pro-Soviet communist), which existed prior to the revolution, with only a handful of them partaking in that upper layer. Castro stood atop the political system, especially before its greater institutionalization in the 1970s, but also even later, albeit often as an arbiter (Brenner, Rose Jiménez, Kirk and LeoGrande 2008, parts I–II; Kapcia 2021, passim). A particular brand of fierce autocratic collectivism, family-based, is found in North Korea and goes on unabated, refusing even economic reform beyond trying at some moments to implement elements of the Chinese model (Kihl and Kim 2006; Izatt 2010).

Here, the issue of the stark personalization of power comes up once again. It happens in all social formations and political regimes, including modern liberal ones, as part of their inner dynamics and logics, not as a perversion, reappearing in authoritarian collectivism (contrary to Lefort 1980b, 121–25). It seems that all societies have to deal, one way or another, with what fills the place of political power, both in modernity and postmodernity thus far. It may be formally rotative and eschew eternal occupiers, regardless of how they eventually fill this space. Modern liberalism and republicanism postulated that power should be exercised abstractly with power holders conceived merely as representatives of the collectivity, sometimes even assembling almost anonymous collectives to achieve this. Socialism, communism and anarchism saw the exercise of power in a similar way, with workers' councils embodying collective power. Yet someone always personally embodies power. This entails a whole series of problems, which modernity and authoritarian collectivism, enmeshed as it is in modernity, have found particularly intractable (if totalitarianism was the former focus of criticism, 'populism' has now substituted it – it seems that the place of power cannot really be left empty).

In the end, none of these regimes was capable of democratization. Perhaps long-term accommodations could have occurred and they could have run for a longer time had they not faced fierce competition with capitalism and corresponding political regimes across the world, more liberal democratic or more authoritarian (Szelenyi and Szelenyi 1994; Runciman 1995). In this vein, the actual evolutionary adaptation they produced rests on the maintenance of their oligarchical or autocratic regimes coupled with the development of capitalism. One could argue, as the Chinese do, that this is merely the first, lower phase of socialism, yet nothing warrants this discourse except unfounded beliefs. Simply because the ruling party calls itself 'communist' does not at all mean that it aims at this sort of future society. Suffice it for now to stress that while there is a truly collective dimension in the political, economic and social life of the former 'real socialism' countries, this never really entailed that they were socialist. We may accept that the development of socialism would not instantly shed income differentials and the differential access to other benefits. Marx ([1875] 1973) adumbrated this in his critique of the programme of German Social Democracy, a point which Stalin seized to argue against egalitarianism. We may also recognize that differences of income and wealth were relatively small in authoritarian collectivism, compared to capitalist countries. Nevertheless, the structure of the state and of the political system precluded their being adequately defined as socialist.

Only democracy could allow any of these states to really be called 'socialist'. Not only because socialism must be defined beyond the economism contained in the simple idea that the end of private property implies the system envisaged by revolutionaries – which, in addition, was strangely seen by twentieth-century Marxism as the only possible successor society to capitalism – but also because real appropriation implies power of command over and enjoyment of the objects which are appropriated. This never happened in any of these countries – not at the economic level, and certainly not at the political level. A *radically democratic political regime* is crucial if a social formation may deserve to be called socialist.

Chapter 7

DEVELOPMENTAL TRENDS

Social systems like those of authoritarian collectivism, which constitute a multifaceted civilization and enjoy long-term existence, all have a genesis, exist for a good while – in this case decades – and eventually disappear. Marx ([1867] 1962; [1894] 1964) pointed to capitalism's historical developmental trends – its 'laws of movement' – and the mechanisms that presided over them: original accumulation, evolution towards the concentration and centralization of capital and simplification of the class structure as well as, eventually, he believed, the expropriation of the expropriators with the proletarian socialist revolution. Other trends were related to the falling rate of profit and capitalism's stagnation – or collapse (*Zusammenbruch*), as Engels and some others read it. The political dimension of modernity – together with capitalism a central component of modern civilization – can be framed according to the same sort of developmental process and mechanisms, implying the strengthening of the state and the political autonomization of individuals (Domingues 2019a, chs 5–6). Can we say the same about authoritarian collectivism? As already observed above, Marcuse (1958, 86–90, 265–67) suggested that the tension between, on the one hand, the emancipatory elements harboured in Marxism, which were present in the ritualized 'Aesopian' language of Soviet Marxism and furnished the ideological linchpin of oppression, and the actual repressive and unequal nature and workings of the whole system on the other, might have eventually proven fatal to it and led to socialism. This did not happen, at least certainly not to the extent necessary and eventually not in a direction which enhanced freedom while preserving socialism.

When the Soviet Union left its satellite states in Eastern Europe, which were much more unstable and were already actually starting to shed the motherland of socialism's model, to their own devices, they quickly turned back to capitalism and traditional forms of the modern liberal state (the latter came about in Russia only very partially, though). Other countries, where the ruling nomenklatura had no intention of following in Gorbachev's footsteps and exiting from history, some of which were already trying to adapt, decided to keep their political systems and political regimes, while at the same time embracing a sort of state capitalism (see Nolan 1995; Anderson 2010). This seemed the only way to avoid extinction.

It is true that Soviet-type societies could have kept developing, had they not faced severe competition with advanced capitalist and politically liberal countries. They could neither force Trotsky's 'permanent revolution' nor keep Stalin's 'socialism in one country', nor even advance with Nikita Khrushchev's 'peaceful coexistence', especially because their competitors and adversaries simply did not take the offer. Mao and Zhou Enlai could afford to be smarter and reach some kind of agreement that eventually allowed, though that was not their intention, for the defeat of the Soviet Union and a return of China to capitalism under Deng Xiaoping a decade later. We thus have trouble identifying inherent tensions and trends within authoritarian collectivism beyond an accumulation of more empirical and disparate elements, even though they can be related to deeper features of the Soviet system, for instance, the relations between the several republics, the union-federation and nationalism (Sakwa 2013). Tensions and trends were really cut short. Yet we can try.

Along with Marcuse's suggestion with respect to the imaginary and the tension between emancipation such as proposed by Marxism and the actual features of the Soviet Union, two other issues emerge. First, the political system saw itself under growing pressure due to both the restriction of freedom and controlled participation within strictly defined limits and the increasingly pointless golden rule of party prominence in all aspects of social life. Time and again the issue surfaced particularly in occupied Eastern Europe, where democratic traditions had been stronger than in Russia prior to the revolution – a limitation that the brief period of radical freedom and egalitarian-grassroots participation in the soviets did not surmount. But all over the countries where the party-state was the cornerstone of the state and of social life, the problem ticked on. It was latent in the Soviet Union, took on huge proportions in the Chinese Cultural Revolution and has been, ever since revolutions took place, a thorny problem for ruling collectivities in authoritarian collectivist societies. Even though the economy evinced problems in the Soviet Union after original accumulation and forced heavy industrialization, whereas nowhere else did the system permit really sustain economic development, it is in the imaginary system of values and norms as well as in the political dimension proper that problems foremost resided.

Take the example of the values of the 1936 Constitution and those which followed it. That constitution set a horizon which created a lot of tension insofar as Soviet citizens had a set of values and norms to which they could appeal (Nathans 2011). Take, furthermore, the interaction of the Soviet state with the idea of human rights, which became increasingly important after the Second World War and was adopted with centrality by the United Nations

(UN) in 1948. Although several authors have stated that the Soviet Union remained aloof and hostile to it – and indeed it did not vote for its adoption in the late 1940s – it did flirt with some of its ideas, and after Khrushchev came to power, the situation utterly changed. Not only did the Soviet state stress the interdependence of rights, civil and political, economic and social, with a particular stress on the right of peoples to self-determination, it tried to connect them to its constitution. According to the Soviet view, the UN Human Rights Declaration of 1948 was only a compromise, while the Soviet Constitution was much more advanced – and indeed, it was the only one to have such an extensive catalogue of 'fundamental rights' (whether or not it respected them). Both government and opposition made recourse to such rights, the former as a means of legitimation which was so important for the Soviet state, with some level of internal publicization during this period. With Brezhnev, however, things changed and this sort of issue was downplayed, according to the period's conservative outlook (Amos 2011).

There was significant incongruity between the values professed about socialism and communism and the actual juridical, political and social conditions of authoritarian collectivism. Tensions were clear, but insufficient to produce real change, since this could threaten and eventually lead to the dislocation of party-state rule. There was some flexibility, but also extensive rigidity. There was, moreover, a sharp separation between the upper strata of the party and state bureaucracy, including managers of companies and the rest of society, that is, Soviet plebeians, who faced a consolidated sort of oligarchic collectivist rule, spanning political, economic and social privilege, even if most of the new oligarchs originated from below. The political system, especially its top layers, was directly responsible for this development and stood as the fiduciary agent of the whole system. It could never allow possible cracks to develop that could jeopardize its integrity, which must have seemed quite fragile to those inside – and remains so, where it has not simply disappeared. Consequently, political control has had to be kept at all costs; otherwise, the system cannot be reproduced.

The generative mechanisms of authoritarian collectivism are directly related to politics. It slowly came about – to the disbelief and incomprehension of several of its founders, from Lenin and Trotsky to Mao and even Ernesto Che Guevara – with the accumulation of power in a revolutionary oligarchy when there had been autochthonous revolutions; in other cases, it was simply transplanted by the Soviet Union. Lenin's lost 'last battle', from his death bed, against Stalin and what he believed constituted the mounting bureaucratic tendencies within the party was a late reflection of this generative mechanism, which set off a trend that Lenin simply could not understand or even recognize as being of his own making (Lewin [1968] 2005).

Take also the Cuban case: the revolution, which originally had no socialist goals, was undertaken by guerrillas who, when they took power (already leading an almost regular army) did not constitute a new sort of participatory power. Instead the revolution relied on the traditional Latin American role of the big leader – or caudillo, if one wants to be nasty – that Castro knew so well how to play. Right from the start, power was concentrated directly in his hands and those of the other guerrilla commanders. They demanded top-down participation, with the creation of a legion of controlled popular organizations, and initially had only the Institute for Agrarian Reform as an institutional apparatus, followed later by the Council of Ministers, initially within a nationalist spirit but soon moving towards 'socialism' (Bengelsdorf 1994). Eventually, all the paraphernalia of Soviet ideology and institutions was imported, and 'real socialism' was normalized as the law of the land with its usual features, though preserving the island's own political dynamic and partial originality (Kapcia 2021, 144ff.). Even if this case epitomizes what can be called poetically the original accumulation of state power in authoritarian collectivism – even though the people who led it had never set this goal for themselves – the Soviet Union was actually the pristine incarnation of the model that was later generalized.

The soviets were indeed an eruption of radical popular democracy in Russia, but in the course of the civil war they quickly declined and were dislocated by an oligarchic ruling group that eventually controlled the Bolshevik party itself and from there the state. The party was itself subordinated to Stalin's autocratic rule and regained prominence only with his death. Yet, no Bolshevik party member would ever think of their actions as oriented to creating a new civilization that was not socialism and would eventually become communism. The melancholy and impatience of the youth in the aftermath of the revolution and 'war communism', a consequence of the civil war, in the placid 1920s, when the country adopted (in a rather consensual manner) the New Economic Policy (NEP) and conciliated with the surviving bourgeois elements, were an expression of this desire to change the world towards proletarian freedom, equality and the end of exploitation. It was about time, they felt, the Soviet Union went beyond what they saw as a wishy-washy moment of accommodation (this may even partly explain the enticement of Stalinism, when the party-state seemingly resumed the expropriation of the exploiters) (Adamczak 2018, 11ff., 77ff.). Policies mirroring war communism re-emerged. Such movement resumed what for many in the party, including already mature leadership, was an important formative period, though the old Bolsheviks were soon liquidated to open room for Stalin's own version of 'socialism', indeed an authoritarian collectivism with one-man rule (Tucker 1999). In this, the centrality of the state was absolute. It had no trenches in what Gramsci ([1929–35] 2001, passim) called 'civil society' and did not govern through it.

The Chinese and the Vietnamese revolutions, highly popular too, developed a similar concentration of power, having already the Leninist sort of party as their model, though they showed greater respect for peasant autonomy. The actually tragic outcome was not even really foreseen by those who produced it, although Mao ([1934] n.d.a; [1966–69] n.d.b; [1970] n.d.c) had always been, ever since the beginnings of the revolutionary process, wary of the power of bureaucracy. Yet even he did not properly understand and define bureaucracy – never, curiously, in particular the party apparatus. In any case, in China at least agrarian reforms were not as centralized and did not harm the peasants as deeply as they did under Soviet forced collectivization. In Vietnam, the party retreated from collectivization due to peasant pressure from below, demonstrating the purportedly more 'dialogical' nature of its political system, in which 'everyday politics' of almost passive resistance had greater influence upon authorities (Kerkvliet 2005, 36, 241).

In all of this, we witness the unintended consequences, unforeseen as well, of the actions of individual revolutionaries and of the moves of their collective organizations unfolding. They took history in directions that were not anticipated, hardly understandable and surely not understood. The theory on which they based themselves, often alongside increasingly meaner interests of course, precluded this. These revolutionaries aimed to establish socialism and usually, especially after the Second World War, national liberation, against colonialism, 'neo-colonialism' and imperialism, which was spearheaded by the United States. China, Vietnam, Cuba, Angola, Mozambique, among others, evince this double revolutionary push. New political structures were meant to correspond to these emancipatory goals. But the way things developed led in a different direction, due to prior 'ideological' commitments and to a specific view of socialism. External capitalist pressure certainly played a role by narrowing the possibilities of experimentation; nevertheless, the interests and values of the new ruling collectivities must not be discounted.

Moreover, we have seen, formerly and now, the open or veiled chauvinism of big nations. This was clear in the case of the Soviet Union almost from the very beginning, and has pertained to China, foremost with Tibet and the Uighurs, till today. A new layer of inequality and domination is thereby established. Lenin was scandalized by this already regarding the brutality with which Georgia was treated by the Russians and Stalin (Lewin, [1968] 2005), but the power structure that he helped build was by no means affected by his misgivings. It is unlikely that things would have been very different had he not died early.

Marxism and the idea that socialism was based fundamentally on the concentration of the means of production in the state and that once economic transformations were achieved ideology and politics would follow suit – that is, the basis conditioned the superstructure –, along with Lenin's rather wishful and largely self-interested (though also well meant) identification of class and party, created an ideological veil that to our day blocks the proper understanding of what had happened. That is, it prevented – and for some still prevents – the recognition of what they were doing, regardless of what they could or were willing to grasp, and what they were instrumental, in an inverted ruse of reason, in engendering. The political dimension of modernity ensued in the revolutionary genesis of authoritarian collectivism. The genetic mechanism was political, basically involving the relatively rapid constitution of the party-state as well as the coupling of politics and ideology with a large bureaucracy, therefore combining political command with administrative command.[1] It was in backward, mostly agrarian, often colonial or semi-colonial and imperialist-dominated countries that the revolutions that led to authoritarian collectivism took place. It was there that this was more likely to happen, especially also because democratic traditions were weaker and exploitation and oppression were stronger. Yet this is not the reason authoritarian collectivism acquired its features: instead, it was the way political power was taken over, organized and stabilized, whereby a new sort of social formation was created, with specific political collectivities at the top (Castoriadis [1964] 1973; Fehér, Heller and Markús 1983, ch. 9).

Marxists never really grasped this unanticipated turn or did so with enormous difficulty, for political and existential reasons, as well as for theoretical ones. Global clashes became increasingly fiercer, the Third World rebelled and nobody wanted to side with capitalism and imperialism. It became painful to accept the tragedy of what socialism and Marxism had come to engender, with the additional risk of being deprived of hope and a vision of the future, as well as of political isolation. The theory, which had helped to partly explain modernity, veiled postmodern reality. In tandem with the long dominant idea of a fixed and limited succession of modes of production, in which socialism/communism out of necessity followed from the socialization of production, which in turn had to have as a corollary the socialization of appropriation, that sort of economism made Marxism helpless in understanding this new social animal.

If the genesis of this new system of rule and its mechanism were political, reiteration of the emerging social formation has the same character. In practice, this meant the unceasing reaffirmation of control and command by the party-state. It could not relinquish it, otherwise it would wither away. It is true that the fear of bureaucracy leading to capitalism – which so many Marxists raised through the years – was not absurd. Indeed, since the 1980s something close to this has been taking place, since the bureaucracy in general to a certain extent is entwined with the political bureaucracy proper. What mattered to this collective system of domination was the reproduction of its own power, based on the collective appropriation of the means of production, yes, but first and foremost the appropriation of the levers of political power, through which that material appropriation could take place. It died out, except where a return to capitalist modernity tout court has taken place, which has happened with the remnants of so-called 'real socialism' taking on different attributes. Top down control endures. For the reasons listed above, given the fragility of the system in terms of legitimation and to a large extent of reproduction – since its explicit ideology and long-term goal contradicted its ordinary existence – it was only through a complicated and distorted relation with its own imaginary, repression, exclusionary political practice, strictly controlled participation and much delusion or cynicism, that the system could work. This eventually drained its energies, though the state in several of these countries was usually capable of keeping things under control.

Furthermore, political centralization in this command society stifled in particular of the economy. It created serious limitations for rational developments. This, too, was due to political expediency, insofar as challenges to official dogma and decisions were at best only partly admitted. Finally, the very opacity of social life became absolute for a state increasingly incapable of seeing through the growing complexity of societal life and, in addition, incapable of making it develop in the direction it putatively wished (that is, economic and technological progress).

In this regard authoritarian collectivism was indeed a dead end (Fehér, Heller and Markús 1983, chs 10–12). This limit and eventual blockage of rationality – which turned, to toy with a Hegelian phrase, into its contrary after a certain stage of development, giving rise to gross irrationality – was apparently impossible to overcome, with capitalism still offering a way out of the stalemate, especially if national liberation had had a paramount role to play in the founding revolution. This does not mean that authoritarian collectivism was doomed from the start and that its final crisis was unavoidable, simply that its contradictions were sharp and far too problematic, particularly in the face of competition by advanced liberal democratic capitalist countries.

What is more, one could argue that the more complex and richer these societies became, the blunter such mechanisms turned out to be, creating problems of 'integration' and commitment to the system (Mouzelis 1993 – drawing upon Parsons' concept of 'societal community'; Sakwa 2013). The impoverished Soviet ideology and its at this stage quasi-utopian imaginary, since it was lost in the distant future, became increasingly hollow within

Brezhnev's technocratic 'developed socialism', after Khrushchev's necessarily failed prognosis of the imminent concretization of communism (Hill 1984; Sandle 2002). On the other hand, participation was too restricted even regarding the interests of important professional groups, although the system did open up to their interference in the 1970s. Again, whatever the problems of liberal democracy – let alone liberalism in its first centuries – competition with its broader mechanisms of political integration was excessively hard to sustain for authoritarian collectivism, whose 'ideologies' also became especially shallow and contradictory. These remain brutal problems for the countries where such political structures survive.

In sum, reproduction of authoritarian collectivism was and had to be directly political, hence always a thorny task. This was above all true of Eastern Europe, but all authoritarian collectivist countries suffered from these problems. Note that all of them were obligated to state, sooner or later, that classes had basically disappeared. They would otherwise be seen as having failed at their own project. On the other hand, the counter-revolution remained a looming threat, according to their proclamations, otherwise repression would make no sense. Reactionary national elements or imperialism were responsible for these problems, not the party-state. This, however, became implausible after socialism had purportedly been built, and just added to the problems of legitimation and self-justification it faced as well as to the reiteration of the patterns of the system as a whole, which was after all never really smooth.

The transformative developmental trends of authoritarian collectivism and the mechanism presiding over them are even more difficult to grasp. Of course, the bosses of the party-state (past and present) would have liked to believe – or at least would have liked others to believe – that communism was being built with the putative socialization of the means of production and the socialization of power (as they affirm it is today). A new democracy was, correspondingly, also in the making, based on the constitutions of all these countries, which in turn reproduced the basic features of the 1936 Stalin Constitution. Competition with the West and economic stagnation, which the 1980s reforms tried to overcome, led to the possibly precocious demise of authoritarian collectivism in its original place of inception. One could argue that the managers had their own interests and had always been a potential incarnation of private capital, hence that it was in their interest that reforms freed them to properly take over these functions. But the rigidity of the system of domination, leaving no room for a smoother relation between the party-state and society, was certainly the key political issue in the breakdown of the Soviet Union and the ensuing demise of almost all the countries of its own camp. China and Vietnam possessed possibly shrewder – and possibly more popularly connected – political oligarchies. Cuba's ruling collectivity was too steeped in Soviet socialism and anti-imperialism to change; nevertheless, it still enjoyed considerable legitimacy, which justified its rule, since it had itself led the revolutionary process with a great deal of support of the population (Domingues [2008] 2011). Moreover, it could not so easily accept something that would be a plain and simple historical defeat. The same was at least partly true of Angola in Africa, though Mozambique and other African countries were too poor to stand international political pressure (Andreas 2001; Pietcher 2002; Domingues, 2012b).

Authoritarian collectivism died of a political disease: the lack of political participation, commitment and trust in its political institutions, with its imaginary at this point also already in tatters, generated a brutal legitimation crisis. It was not economic failure, despite problems of performance in the face of huge progress in the West, which produced its downfall.

There is one case – inconclusive, however – that could challenge this line of argument: the evolution of Czechoslovakia in the 1960s (Sik 1971; Golan 1971). For a good while important currents within the party pushed for change, which at least at the highest point of what became a powerful national movement had democratization at its core, alongside more market-oriented reforms. This party was never willingly and entirely grounded in the Third International model, that is, it was more reformist between the two world wars. A sort of 'democratic socialism' was envisaged, at least around 1968, entailing even the end of the party-state structure. The process went much further than the spasmodic and limited attempts at reform, as well as working class revolts, which took place in Poland, Hungary and East Germany. Implying organized plans and procedures, it came to have the backing of large swathes of both the Czech and the Slovenian populations. The astonishing changes were brutally interrupted by the 'Warsaw Pact'–Soviet invasion. We thus do not know if the project would have been successful. This might have entirely transformed the configuration of 'real socialism', democratizing it, at least in the region. Maybe. But things might have been aborted by an internal coup – the party-state had reserves which served it well in the aftermath of the crisis – or simply moved towards some sort of social democratic-cum-state capitalism, with eventual changes in foreign policy, though in principle these were never tabled. An internal coup would have been less painful for the region's party-states; the other possibilities, they could not at all allow to bloom. The history of Czechoslovakia and the Communist Party there may have been responsible for that unexpected opening, along with a serious crisis that seems to have befallen the country in the early part of the decade as well (Jancar 1971).

Yet since the process was aborted, the beautiful Prague Spring works merely as a partial counterfactual possibility of development, a nice one indeed, yet impossible to verify. It is unlikely to be repeated elsewhere, as in particular China's evolution has shown, epitomized by the mobilization of the Chinese youth up to the Tiananmen Square 'incident', with its violence and tragic outcome (Dingxin 2001). Gorbachev's fate tells the same tale, though in a different way. In both cases, we see reformist factions emerge that could not carry the day. Since it did surface in different countries and occasions, it seems that this was by no means due to sheer contingency – contrary to what Castoriadis ([1987] 1990) suggested, who was beset by the rigidity of his own theses about the Soviet Union. On the other hand, these reforms, blocked from within, with different outcomes or crushed from without, could never progress towards a more democratic social form. Capitalism, with the demise or the adaptation of the party-state, has always been the upshot of collective authoritarianism.

Chapter 8

AUTHORITARIAN COLLECTIVISM AND CAPITALISM TODAY

We have seen above that it is difficult to discern which exactly were the developmental trends at work within authoritarian collectivism, insofar as they ended rather suddenly. Indeed, they probably ended before the system exhausted its developmental possibilities. The economy had problems, but these led to some desperation only due to the competition of the Soviet Union with the West, which showed much greater strength and innovative capacity. Politically, relations were fraught, but if reforms were not undertaken the system could have survived for longer or even a very long time. Once there was an opening it quickly became crystal clear that if the genie was out of the bottle and political tensions ran their course unimpeded, authoritarian collectivism could not survive. And in fact it did not survive – not in the Soviet Union and not in the countries more directly connected to it when they had no true autonomous revolutionary process behind them. Even those that did, such as Yugoslavia, which moreover had a more supple and participatory economic system as well as less repression, could not stick to 'real socialism' in the ambience of change that overwhelmingly prevailed in Eastern Europe. In Africa, surrender was far-reaching. It was only in Asia and in a small Latin American country that successful attempts to survive were rolled out.

If we focus on the economic side, it was the blockages that over-centralization produced once heavy industrialization was accomplished that were a developmental problem. The sort of planning practised was highly defective. Low frequency signals, which a more decentralized (market-oriented or network-based) economy could provide, were lost in the top-down model adopted since Stalin and partly even before him, despite the formidable war machinery it was able to build and the growing welfare it managed to provide the Soviet working class, especially during the 1980s (Nove [1983] 1991; Blackburn 1991). Consumer goods for dispersed individual consumers and high technology were hardly achievable goals. 'Relations of production' and 'productive forces' clashed, whether there was a possibility to surpass the blockage within the 'mode of production' or not. In the end, it was the complicated intertwinement of political and economic conditions that further generated what became insurmountable contradictions.

The Chinese watched carefully the demise of the Soviet Union and decided that, in order to keep the rule of the party-state, no democratic opening should be truly allowed. On the other hand, relations of production at the economic level should change and property partly pluralized; capitalism should thus be adopted, but the state structure must be left intact to highest degree possible. This trend became even stronger after the Tiananmen Square tragedy, in which a complicated political showdown and fierce repression occurred, involving divisions in society, state and party. The hold of the party-state and its oligarchy has since become dogma in order that nothing similar happens again. The process entailed, however, a shift in the elements of legitimation of the party-state and the political regime, as well as some democratization at the lowest levels. If formerly it was revolutionary ideology and Marxist–Leninist–Mao Zedong thought that mattered, now economic performance became paramount. Consequently, the role of the party is framed in terms of efficiency in pursing and fulfilling the goals of fast development and enrichment, with villages being allowed some self-management (see, for local elections, O'Brien and Han 2009). Some would argue, abroad only, it seems that the old 'Mandate of Heaven' underpins and buttresses the party-state legitimacy (Shue 2004), but surely economic performance predominantly matters. Vietnam followed suit, with the Moi Doi reforms, more modest, keeping the role of the party within the party-state, but also changing the economy (including privatization – actually leasing – of land and eventually its concentration to nourish agribusiness production, foreign dominated). Cuba has been taking longer, but more recently has accelerated economic reforms, including formally relinquishing democratic centralism in the 1992 Constitution (though not in practice) and the 2019 Constitution, without ever questioning the centrality of the party-state. The coronavirus pandemic put even more pressure on the whole system.

Nationalism lies at the core of all the imaginary of these countries, which eventually combined with socialism–communism as well as the Leninist model of party and the application of the democratic centralism framework. In all these countries overcoming foreign oppression, or 'imperialism', was absolutely central for the revolution and its later legitimation. Nationalism was a main revolutionary driving force; eventually, it is what has mostly remained.

Political command and partly bureaucratic, administrative command have therefore kept the upper hand in these societies, with inflections in the system of rule and its elements of legitimacy. Yet they have travelled a long way, or are in the process of taking such a road, from authoritarian collectivism to capitalism with much of the state format maintained – though not all of it. The political system has retained some key characteristics, such as the centrality of the party and democratic centralism, with a particularly important role reserved for censorship and political repression, carried out by the political police or less important police bodies. Communist oligarchy is at the core of China's, Vietnam's, Laos's and now Cuba's political system, whereas North Korea perseveres in its autocratic collectivist and dynastic regime, which, some would argue, harks back to traditional Confucian family views, still operative in the country. The ruling collectivities have carefully gauged their steps in order not to lose control, repression assuming variable intensity at different moments, with controlled participation having by now all but faded. In China, this general move gave rise to a model of 'layered authoritarianism'. 'Princelings' – politicians whose family have connections to former revolutionary cadres – are particularly important in the reiterated political system. Furthermore, the party-state is now cut across by 'special interests' and deeply embedded in market activities (Wang 2009, xxviii, xxxi–xxxii). The principles of nomenklatura and those of class division in capitalism – a complex, multi-sized bourgeoisie and a large proletariat, with a huge peasantry inhabiting the countryside – have been mixed, complementing each other, despite tensions and struggles.

More recently, China has developed into an even more autocratic and repressive political regime, with widespread surveillance and control, under general secretary Xi Jinping. Having inherited a rather developed capitalist economic system – although China is still a 'middle-income country', despite the absolute size of its economy – which in a few decades entirely changed the domestic and international landscape and with a particularly successful project of modernization, he is now moving the country in a new direction. The state must become economically stronger and militarily powerful. Alongside greater international assertiveness (whether this will really work is open to doubt), Xi has decisively restrengthened the party-state, repression and nationalism, 'democratic centralism' and discipline. 'Collective leadership' is gone and there is now even Xi Jinping Thought, with no limits for his term in power (Garrick and Chang Bennett 2018; Economy 2019, especially chs 2–3).

There is no Orientalist assumption – which, moreover, overlooks how democratic centralism persists at the core of the political system as well as minimizes repression and censorship – that might turn the lack of democracy into a virtue, normatively, as if a sort of neo-Confucian 'meritocracy' could be an alternative. This would have been already partially implemented, as argued by Bell and Pei (Bell [2015] 2016; Pei 2017; Bell and Pei 2020, ch. 2). Bell himself has actually become less committed to democracy. Formerly, he conceived of a traditional bureaucratic chamber alongside a democratically elected one (Bell 2008); now, he and Pei have dismissed the democratic element from their 'China model' altogether, becoming highly apologetic of the regime, expressing only minor criticism. His former model, which had already formed a part of the so-called 'new Confucian' revival (Domingues [2010] 2011), was similar to Sun Yat-sen's ([1924] 1999) proposal to combine Western and Chinese philosophies, the results of which purportedly orient Taiwan's state institutions. Sun's ideal regime would thus have combined popular democratic rights, corresponding to 'political power' (*Chun Ch'uan*) and five 'administrative powers' (*Chi Ch'uan*) of government, which featured those formed through 'popular will' – legislative, executive, judiciary – as well as the 'examining power' and 'supervisory power', the power of 'experts', since people are usually stupid ('unthinking', as he put it), have no 'political ability' and are not fit to exercise 'political responsibility'. Now Bell and Pei fall behind even that, though they certainly do not argue that people are stupid.

Instead of collapsing bureaucratic–meritocratic (whether of a Confucian–Legalist sort or rational-legal Western) and political command, we need to distinguish between them. In reality, China's political system is in this regard not very different from former technocratic rule in the Soviet Union, from Brezhnev's 'developed socialism' period onwards. It simply functions, more efficiently, in a larger and more complex society, possibly with some elements of Confucian mentality, despite other features at the local level. The party is, on the other hand, closer to the Kuomintang in terms of a nationalist modernizing project, although it rhetorically remains within the Marxist–Leninist fold (as did the nationalist organization). Even at the local level, democratization has faced many hurdles (Perry and Goldman 2007). Similar arguments could be raised regarding Vietnam and Laos, though Confucianism is not as central in their history. The state-party-cum-capitalist path characterizes them, possibly with more social embeddedness, more conflict and actual political pluralism in the Vietnamese case, with the party possibly grappling with more trouble too (Kerkvliet, Tria, Russell and Koh 2003; Gainsborough 2010; London 2014; Creak and Barney 2018; To, Mahanty and Wells-Dang 2019).[1]

This has led to, and has been coupled with, a return to modernity, which has not, however, discarded the experiment of 'real socialism' at the political level. The latter remains, with variable importance, a sort of empty imaginary goal, with no links to praxis, along with a Marxism that makes very little sense. The state attempts to mobilize Confucianism in particular in China as a legitimation complement, along with nationalism and sheer utilitarian economic performance, in all these countries. This partly explains the longevity of these regimes. Not by chance do the armed forces have – or used to have – such a huge influence in these countries. Corruption, a big problem in all of them, save for Cuba, apparently has the opposite effect, an issue that purportedly underlies Xi's authoritarian and cleansing push. On the other hand, political inequality and socio-economic inequality, the deeper the capitalist development has advanced in them, now go hand in hand. In turn, this model does not represent a mere return to the 'industrial society', as if Durkheim was now vindicated, and only political adaptations had taken place. Instead, what we are dealing with here is a far-reaching change of socio-economic structures.

Greater change than in the political system as such can be found in the partial overhaul of the judicial system of these countries, save Cuba's, while China has also more recently moved back and strengthened the prerogatives of the party. This is a topic of keen interest in the literature, much more than the legacy of the political system of authoritarian collectivism. Even if in all of the states where this system existed the Stalin juridical legacy still predominates, some adaptation to 'human rights' ideas has been introduced, to which governments pay mostly lip service. At the same time, the security of private property has become a deep concern of legal reforms, despite the party-state large-scale control of property and appropriation, and the continued dominance of the party (Yu 1989; Pérez-Stable 1999; Peerenboom 2002; Gillespie 2004; Lin 2006; Mo 2010; Samsónov and Días Torres 2014; Hualing, Gillespie, Nicholson and Parlett 2018; Bartot Tirana 2019; Kapcia 2021).[2] The nomenklatura has not by any means disappeared, but now it is complemented by the emergence of a truly capitalist class: while China dubiously claims to have eliminated poverty, inequality has soared to levels close to those of the United States (Piketty, Li and Zucman 2019). Mao was thus wrong about the role of bureaucracy in reintroducing capitalism. It was the party that brought it back to life, in its own interest to survive, which the former backward economics of state socialism could not guarantee.

This was possible, however, contrary to Mao's understanding and actual personal indulgence, because the party-state system of rule, on the one hand, and capitalism as a system of class domination, on the other, were able to fuse in a smoothly-run double-edged system of domination, despite tensions and with the advantage of a specific ideological cover. Particularly within China itself, but in the other countries discussed here too, this makes it harder to obtain an adequate view of the real dynamics and developmental trends of this sort of blend. It includes political and bureaucratic hierarchies and command as well as expanded market relations and voluntary exchange, not to mention its mix of nomenklatura and capitalist class (with a minor role, except in advanced technological areas of the economy, being played by networks and voluntary collaboration) (Domingues 2012, ch. 4). It now also mixes capitalism's 'laws of movement' such as discussed by Marx – though for the time being well-administered by the party-state – and, despite features specific to such political systems, those that pertain to a political constitution, authoritarian collectivism, that tried to break free from modernity. This was a truly amazing historical turnabout, whose destiny – whatever it is – is still to be seen.

Of course, one could bring up the NEP interlude in the Soviet Union to make the point that it is simply a sensible return to something similar to that experience that is re-emerging. But the NEP was something different, at least contextually. It was an attempt, by an extremely backward society, in the aftermath of civil war in the early 1920s, to achieve a minimal balance, favouring economic development and a truce with the peasantry. We do not know if it would have produced a Chinese model *avant la lettre*, though it could have, if it had persisted in the long run, superimposed a nomenklatura onto a capitalist economy, with a strong presence of the state, since, to start with, capitalism was indeed at its core. This might justify the talk of the Chinese ruling circles of a 'first phase of socialism'. What we see today is different, though. Contemporary reforms are responses to the failures of command economies, led by parties long entrenched in power and looking for legitimation and survival, in the midst of a new phase of modernity, with staggering technological development and the hegemony, at least until the early 2020s, of a neoliberal outlook.

Only equality and network horizontality between citizens can underpin and buttress democracy, not hierarchies based on knowledge or superior capacity. The latter are just what democracy aimed to combat and which philosophy, since Plato and later in the West, has far too often tried to re-establish. Confucianism cannot be, by definition, a solution in this regard, nor can the simple idea that hierarchies are justified by the 'service' those above provide those below. Of course, some sort of layered authority might be really necessary in extremely large and complex societies (Habermas 1981). Governmental efficiency is desirable in order that things get done and correspond, in terms of output, to democratic decision-making processes. Not wasting energy and practically responding to the expectations that decisions taken are implemented is part and parcel of democracy. Yet one should not mistake political decisions and ensuing commands for bureaucratic power. Both need to be controlled, even if it is often difficult to distinguish between them. The former must count on citizen participation, directly or indirectly, beyond even the Maoist 'mass line' in which hierarchy hardly gives in to the autonomous participation of such masses, since the party always stands above them. This is a point made long ago by anarchists, who foresaw the danger that hierarchies of knowledge presented for socialism and democracy (Bakunin [1983] 1990, 177ff.). A Kuomintang–Communist–Confucian aristocracy only makes this knowledge hierarchy worse.

If understanding the trajectory of 'real socialism', in reality authoritarian collectivism, is important in itself and for what a socialist project might still be, it is also extremely relevant for understanding and demystifying the remnants of 'Soviet-type' societies. As the attempt at the construction of a new sort of society faltered and was eventually eliminated, still ruling communist oligarchies have carefully trod this transition to a sort of state capitalism (although the extremely autocratic character of North Korea seems to preclude even that). There are die-hards in all these countries, which, for instance, in Cuba until 2021 partly held the process back, even though individual 'entrepreneurs' (traditional Latin American *cuentapropismo*) mushroomed long ago. These die-hards are wont to retain the old fusion of state and economy, public and private, which has been giving way to a more traditionally modern division, although command maintains its grip on society politically and partly economically. This is what has been left of – and for – them as a strategy of survival in evolutionary terms.

In none of these countries has 'socialism', in the form of state property and stark restrictions to the market, survived beyond the possible goodwill and delusions of some intellectuals and party cadres, whether in a neo-Stalinist, ever weaker, or in participatory-socialist terms or as neo-Maoism, which have no political clout. But Marxism–Leninism lives on, as an institutional strategy of collectivities that were skilled enough to lose their rings but keep their fingers. Perhaps some of them still believe in socialism. It is true, too, that history has ideas and imaginary constellations as crucial elements for its unfolding. But reality demands its share, and if ideas can become a revolutionary force, in the cases we have been discussing here it will certainly be against those who formally and collectively profess them – if they still do – that such revolutionary processes will have to be waged, save for individual exceptions.

If we contemplate the global scene, things are disquieting, too. This is particularly clear in what regards the fate of human rights under the Chinese regime. The growing level of repression and human rights abuse stems from Xi's autocratic ascension. But the problems go further, touching the international level. China, as a poor and then middle-income country struggling to overcome its predicament, is highly sensitive to criticisms in this area, and it has stressed the superiority of economic and social rights over and above the civil and political level, with a starkly statist reading of the 'right to development'. More seriously, it has tried to sell its own version of human rights and skew the workings of the United Nations in this respect. It has promoted those priorities by rhetorically differentiating human rights under 'socialism with Chinese characteristics' (a phrase very similar to ideas related to so-called 'Asian values') from the 'Western' way of understanding human rights. What that actually means is at best very obscure. Finally, China has decided to play a particular role within the UN human rights regime, especially in the Human Rights Council (which substituted the Human Rights Commission). It has sided with a 'like-minded' group of countries, as it is called, which includes Russia, Pakistan, India, Belarus, Bangladesh but also, surely, Cuba, Vietnam and Venezuela. Along with them, China has worked to distort the Council procedures, sap its institutional foundations, change norms in order to weaken them and limit its activity (Yu-Jie 2019).

It is in any case interesting to raise the question whether at least part of the developmental trends of authoritarian collectivism remains operative. Even if economic, utilitarian performance is now a paramount element of legitimation in these party-state systems, insofar as they profess faith in socialism, the former contradiction between ideas and reality has not entirely vanished, although it has surely been attenuated and a more cynical attitude has set in, with nationalism abetting it. How it will unfold in the long run we can only guess, though in this regard Bell and Pei are correct: nobody seems to believe inside China that it still has anything to do with socialism. On the other hand, the bottleneck of over-centralization, which blocked economic development beyond heavy industrialization, was overcome by the adoption of capitalism, with a model which is a key component of what can be globally called 'flexible and polarized accumulation' (Domingues 2012, ch. 6). That being said, uninterrupted growth has been crucial to the Chinese regime, but it cannot last forever.

Chapter 9

SOCIALISM AND COMMUNISM

All of this begs the question, where then can we place authoritarian collectivism, evolutionarily and politically? Its failure was an unheard-of historical blunder, apparently without parallel. Other projects of total change usually accrued to individual destines out of this world, in the 'beyond' of spiritual life. Others were more closely related to processes that were already unfolding in social life, such as those put forward by radical Protestant sects in America or Calvin's rule in Zurich. Communism was supposed to be such a project, but it was much more ambitious. Its dreams were, however, carefully distinguished from utopianism, especially in that Marx and Engels ([1848] 1978; Marx [1867] 1962) identified economic and social developmental trends within capitalism and modernity overall – in the contradiction between social, capitalist accumulation and private appropriation, entailing class structure and conflict. In their view, these trends should lead in a more or less straightforward manner to socialism and then communism. Marx's extreme confidence in his scientific understanding of those trends assured him that this was the only possible evolution from the stage humanity had reached, capitalism supposedly representing the last 'antagonistic' social formation (Marx [1859] 1971). When placed within a unilinear perspective of evolution, presupposed by the mainstream of Marxism until the recovery – problematically staged – of the 'Asiatic mode of production' in the second half of the twentieth century, socialism and communism were inexorably on the agenda, even though they had to be brought about by historical agents.

Both doctrine and practice, however, present problems that conspired to push, rather hard, away from the cherished goal. The doctrine suffered from the identification of those trends, particularly regarding class evolution (indeed a simplification) and the outcome of class struggle (the consciousness of the proletariat and the choice to end exploitation and oppression) that, out of necessity, were seen as entailing an emancipated society. The problems of practice stemmed from revolution occurring only in economically very backward countries, to start with Russia, furnishing a model that was not actually exportable to more advanced ones. That being said, it *was* imaginarily exported and forced on workers' organizations more deeply committed to socialism in advanced capitalist countries, even though revolution was defeated across Europe. This defeat was compounded by the cold shoulder given to revolution by most workers, either because there was really no reason to expect it in Europe and the United States or because outcomes elsewhere and ruling collectivities' responses in the West made it less attractive for what should have been, according to the theory, the revolutionary proletariat.

It is not my intention to discuss this in detail here, but it seems clear that authoritarian collectivism, travestied as socialism, was both a force and a hindrance to the development of socialism worldwide. Especially in the 'underdeveloped' world, it energized and often directed the struggle against imperialism and colonialism (Gallissot 1981), with victories that made a number of nations fairly proud. More than anyone else and with great suggestiveness, Lenin politically theorized this twentieth-century strategic perspective. But 'real socialism' was not a very enticing reality, even if one discounted the nasty capitalist encirclement the Soviet Union and other anti-imperialist revolutions, Cuba above all, suffered, especially due to the United States' counter-revolutionary policies. It had serious political limitations, even though, economically, the record varies from country to country and could, maybe, have been made better in the long-run, had it not foundered or undergone a transition to a form of state capitalism. Its political system was excessively rigid and closed. In an age in which democracy and the affirmation of plebeian and citizen political demands as such were mounting – and keep mounting today still – it's at best oligarchic, at worst, autocratic character, with a great deal of repression, a crucial role for censorship and the political police, (purportedly) disguised by only a thin democratic veil, could not withstand the criticisms that eventually made it an illegitimate social formation. This happened both inside and outside the countries it existed.

In any case, a truce in the fierce political clashes of the interwar period and concessions were achieved, lasting for some decades in the second half of the twentieth century. In a sort of boomerang effect, the Soviet constitutions also influenced European countries once the Second World War was over (though in the West of divided Germany the constitutionalization of social rights present in the Weimar document was abandoned). Italy, in particular, exemplifies this impact. Its new post-war Constitution defined it as a 'republic of labour' (though not of 'toilers', as in the Italian Communist Party's initial proposal such as laid down by Togliatti), with a consistent list of social rights (Urbinati 2017). After the debacle of the 1990s, the political and social situation became much worse, compounded by the rise of neoliberalism.

Nevertheless, we witness today renewed interest in socialism and communism. The issue of power – how to arrive and stay there, but at the same time maintain radical democracy – has come to the forefront and a debate carries on about whether parties can be paramount instruments, or whether more spontaneous action is required; some, on the other hand, have returned to the very meaning and programme of socialism (Badiou 2009; Honneth, 2015; Dean 2016; Arato 2019; Sunkara, 2019).[1] Whether the project of true emancipation, in which the entwinement of freedom, equality and solidarity, the care for 'nature' and different ways of engaging with oneself and the world come about, will still be called socialism, let alone communism, may be open to doubt. Changing names does not actually amount to a solution and may be seen as a poor device to reignite a perspective that had a bad go in actual practice. In any case, a thorough critique of 'real socialism' is necessary. Firstly, we need to revise what authoritarian collectivism meant, with its true collective nature and authoritarian political structure, which prevented it from evolving in an emancipatory direction, as well as, more positively, led it to build increasingly broad welfare systems. What happens in the political dimension is in itself – and not merely instrumentally – fundamental and has far-reaching consequences, including political inequality, which can easily transit into socio-economic inequality.

How power and democracy can be joined is still an unanswered issue for socialist perspectives. This is a problem that has been at the centre of socialist/communist politics since the Paris Commune, the Bolshevik Revolution, May 1968 and the Cultural Revolution, let alone innumerable demonstrations and movements since the early 2010s. This is also what Badiou (2003; 2009) has perceptively stressed, although he saw Mao's role as being of a symbolic and unifying character, wrongly downplaying his position as the big boss of a current within the party that hardly had further democratization in mind, finally using the army against former allies when he thought necessary. We do not know how to solve this problem. It has little to do with bureaucracy, contrary to what many on the Left are prone to believe. Bureaucratic hierarchies and mentality can indeed have harmful effects; nevertheless, bureaucracy as such is not only inevitable in highly complex societies, but also sometimes a relief in most daily dealings, as long as it is fair, democratically controlled and dedicated to serving citizens. In any event, an answer to this question will surely not be found with a return either to traditional authoritarian collectivist alternatives or with the apology of supposedly meritocratic Confucian legitimation.

To be sure, as an anti-imperialist project, guaranteeing the autonomy of nations that agonized under foreign rule or were threatened by it, the communist project was extremely effective in many places, more so than liberal and/or capitalist alternatives, which were themselves usually also very authoritarian. But it is here that critique must once again intervene. The countries that emerged from the anti-colonial and/or anti-imperialist struggle – once legion, for instance in Africa – and persist with the political forms of authoritarian collectivism – still try to legitimate themselves internally and even externally (as Cuba does in Latin America) by wearing the shabby socialist garb they once exhibited. This becomes increasingly absurd as political authoritarianism blends with capitalism, exploitation and social inequality. While the former imaginary of these societies included an emancipatory horizon, as distorted as it was, the new directions rest on capitalism and enrichment, entailing legitimation by performance, without giving up the highly hierarchical state and political structure. We must not close our eyes to this. Of course, this does not mean siding with imperialism and the threats which the United States, though not alone, presents to these countries, with their odious blockages and embargos. Neither solution is acceptable. We must find a way to fight imperialism without falling victim to the sort of blackmail Stalinism has put forward so many times, ridiculously resumed in the accusation that criticizing and not supporting these regimes is tantamount to choosing the side of reactionaries and foreign intervention.

Venezuela under and post Hugo Chávez, with his Socialism for the Twenty-First Century, offers a picture that is no less bleak (Lander 2016; 2020, 121–24; Lopez Maya 2016). It is true that the United States' pressure and internal bourgeois resistant has been fierce, that geopolitics has been played against it, though less severely than it was against the Cuban Revolution. This certainly blocked smoother developments of its reformist and at its height very popular process. But the country never overcame (or even really tried) its total dependency on oil exports (the 'magic state', according to a famous book), as of late just adding mining – under military control – to its primarized economy, with a stark personalization of politics and a top-down push. Moreover, the construction of the so-called 'communal state' has been highly problematic. It simply reproduced past authoritarian (collectivist) models, based as it is on Cuban institutions, experience and advice, which Chavism freely chose. Centralization at the top and controlled mobilization are its mainstays, starting with the United Socialist Party of Venezuela (PSUV), created by Chavez with Castro's impulse and characterized by democratic centralism (for a positive view, see Raby 2006). This framework left behind more open societal forms of popular participation included in the first Bolivarian Constitution promulgated by Chavez, in favour of a traditional twentieth-century sort of 'real socialism' institutional format. It was actually not approved in the referendum called by Chavez, but he later all the same deviously implemented the changes, speaking of Socialism for the Twentirth-First Century.

From the very beginning, Chavez's personal power promoted and at the same time curtailed autonomous popular initiative, which, having formerly thrived, the new constitution has radically subordinated; at the same time, military power and widespread corruption have contaminated the whole of social and political life. Even if the opposition resumes the worst sort of pro-US reactionary liberalism typical of much of Latin American history, this does not excuse the path Chavism has taken. This once again fundamentally evinces the stubborn attachment of the Latin American left to worn-out models (including the perennial return to extractivism).

It is regrettable to see other political formations move towards this sort of mould and display similar authoritarian leanings. One such case has been that of the Movimiento al Socialismo (MAS) in Bolivia as well (Tapia and Chavez 2020). Stemming from powerful mobilizations and community-based organizations of indigenous peoples, a top-down mentality in a Stalin–Leninist mould combined with Latin American strong personalization came to the fore once the party assumed power. Its ruling circle, to start with Evo Morales and Álvaro García Linera, autocratically tried to stay there beyond their constitutional periods, and managed the party's relations with social organizations vertically, trying to exert control and exclude critical voices. Although the process is still in flux, it seems that, after a political crisis, when Morales was forced to step down, and a short period of right-wing government, the hopes for an overhaul that might lead the MAS to renew itself and become more democratic will not be fulfilled in the aftermath of the party's massive victory in the 2020 elections.

Chapter 10

LOOKING INTO THE FUTURE

The last words of this book must be reserved for the uncountable people who militated in parties and movements that led to these socio-political systems, supported or even in good faith staffed them. This includes others who, like Trotskyites, criticized them but could not think of revolutions that would not reproduce the problems that made of them an oppressive rather than an emancipatory reality. Surely there have been those who were cynical as well as misguided or prone to delusion. But there were also those, and they were legion, who were dedicated and believed that the future would be bright once class society and private property were abolished, despite the price paid in the transitional period. These were people who sided with the wretched of the earth and took upon themselves sometimes personally dangerous and difficult, even brutal, decisions, with the dream of a society free from exploitation and oppression in the hope that, as Brecht poetically put it, those who were born later would forgive them for their harshness. Far too often they made mistakes and committed unjustifiable acts, but far too often did they do so in good faith, in the midst of complicated historical processes. The situation is no longer the same, history has moved on and the shortcomings of such a perspective are now plain to see.

Just after the Second World War (partly under the influence of debates about French resistance heroes and collaborationists, and in fact siding to a large extent with Stalinist arguments, with a sort of consequentialist ethic), Merleau-Ponty ([1947] 1951, particularly 3–4) thought it possible that even the Moscow Trials could truly make sense – could be justified indeed – to communists. He thought that within Marxism, the outcomes of decisions – right or wrong – could acquire an objectivity that implied a sort of personal responsibility for agents, in which revolutionary violence and terror found a place, though extraordinary if compared with other historical circumstances. Future outcomes of a history in the making were somehow the judge of the present, in which actors in a strange retrospective/prospective manner could find themselves wrong. Moreover, he argued that liberalism was not innocent of violence either, in fact even under ordinary circumstances. Although the latter is undoubtedly true, today we can no longer accept his fairly positive (and naïve) evaluation of Stalinism: there is no historical rationality which forecloses history and can – according to the understanding of a closed oligarchy, irrespective of its self-proclamation as the party of the proletariat – define, in the absence of an actual future, which is the correct political line. Even if we think of a politics of the extraordinary, such teleological and terrorist methods must be definitively rejected. And even if we could still hold fast to such standards, the judgement of history has falsified the political choices taken in the course of 'real socialism', leading to its radical defeat and loss of historical horizons, yet not to the end of violence.

Today, some cling to past, failed solutions for lack of imagination and immediatism. Stalinism still casts a 'long shadow' over the Left (Jünke 2007). Arguments of expediency abound in this connection. Indeed, they were originally why Lenin was connected to Jacobinism (a charge he partly, perhaps provocatively, gladly accepted, adding his, at the time, 'social democratic' commitment to it – Lenin [1904] 1964), despite the (too) many differences that cannot be overlooked. While these arguments are of course not entirely false, what efficacy means has to be asked and not supposed or explained away, especially when we reckon with the disaster of democratic centralism and authoritarian collectivism, as well as look at the world today, in which demands of self-organization have become even stronger. Others imagine themselves as powerful leaders within a social formation similar to historical authoritarian collectivism, while still others exercise the sort of power democratic centralism allows for in the sort of verticalized schemes that are typical of Leninist parties which Trotskyism curiously embraced, too, notwithstanding Trotsky's prior dislike of centralism. Ideology is at play here, and an authoritarian mentality often lurks beneath such outlooks, though some already know better and only partly embrace such perspectives (for instance, trying to lend democratic centralism a genuinely democratic character).

The remnants of Stalinism must therefore be brought into the open and criticized. Latin America in particular is a prisoner to this old imaginary. This is bound to produce disasters, partly due to a brutal *consequentialist* view of political solutions, that is, that ends justify means, whatever they might be and how intensely and extensively they were applied. This has led to regular demoralization since often means are bad as such and eventually become ends, with the mere desire to stay in power often underpinning supposedly noble intentions. Even when they are noble, the problem surfaces time and again, since this may be totally overrun by the meanness of means.

The problem, however, beyond individual and collective shortcomings as well as even mean material and political interests, was – and what lingers of it is – rooted in the conceptions and premises, simplistic at that, within which the Left historically developed. We need to overcome them, and to do this it is still, or once again, necessary to seriously take stock of the heritage of the Left.

Yet what we need is far more than (even) that. It is necessary to discover in current social processes the trends that may take us beyond modernity. As noted above, Marx and Marxism located this in the economic sphere and the 'laws of movement' of capitalism with its process of accumulation. We can, however, spot it in the political dimension proper as well – and this is precisely the demand for social and political autonomy, alongside self-determination, that modernity has increasingly imposed on political systems that have more recently become increasingly oligarchic and count on a state that has become stronger and stronger. In the long run, radical democracy and socialism cannot but go hand in hand (Domingues 2019a). We must move away from any form of technocratic Saint-Simonian persuasion, even if travestied with Marxism, and recognize that autocratic and oligarchical problems beset contemporary politics. The experience of councils – Soviets and the like – is relevant, but it must not be reified: we must be open to new forms and possibilities. What is more, we must not simply pretend to efface the conquests of modernity and also liberalism – equal freedom and universalist law, supposedly entwined but in fact hurt by a phony top-down 'socialist legality' in the trajectory of authoritarian collectivism. We must retrace this path.

If socialism is to have a second chance on the face of the earth, we therefore need to separate clearly what it can be from what it once supposedly was, despite the good intentions and bravery of so many past socialists and communists. This is how socialism can be made attractive once again and, banking on the desires of citizens and the social processes they push forward, can be made an unprecedented historical reality of horizontally networked citizens of a planetary, complex and advanced civilization. For those who envisage radical social change, there should be no serious reason not to embrace its renewal.

NOTES

Chapter 1 Authoritarian Collectivism and the Political Dimension

1 This book, in this respect, is concerned with issues similar to those Rigby (1964) grappled with in his confused and excessively concrete distinction, offering a more precise analytical approach.

2 Fehér (1987) in particular gave expression to the concerns of this group of authors with Jacobinism, implicitly identifying the French with the Russian Revolution. There was indeed much 'politicism' in both revolutions, that is, an effort to force history in a specific direction and accelerate it through the deployment of political power, a problem ingrained in the evolution of Marxist praxis since Marx (who disliked Jacobinism) and above all Lenin. Yet speaking of the Russian Revolution and especially of 'Soviet-type' societies in terms of Jacobinism is excessive. See Ingram (2018); Domingues (2019b).

3 If his Marxist assessment was accompanied by extreme Left, in fact rather naive, political positions, then the later pages in Castoriadis's (1981) work are surely the worst he ever wrote. They unfortunately reproduce radical right-wing Cold War discourses. He stressed the supposed role of the military as eventually the dominant force in the Soviet Union (characterized as a 'stratocracy'), the putatively expansionist character of its foreign policy and of Russian chauvinism, including an allegedly military superiority of the Soviet Union and the supposedly 'dual character' of Soviet society (in which the only modern sector was the military). In any case, while we can hardly find expansionist policies by 'socialist' countries and speaking of a Soviet 'empire' makes little sense, the Russians did build a defence belt in Eastern Europe. Furthermore, to some extent political domination – consonant with what is argued here at length – was at the core of their relations with other communist countries and parties, for a long time keeping them subordinate to the foreign policy and security interests of the Soviet Union. See Grigot (2005).

4 Arendt ([1951] 1973, 323) explained the rise of Nazism referring to the previous atomization of the masses, though offering no empirical support for this statement. She then supposedly 'explained' Stalin's totalitarianism with his need to atomize the masses, therefore not atomized before his rise, with a bizarre inversion of causality.

Chapter 2 Political Command: The Elementary 'Cell-Form'

1 Weber ([1921–22] 1980, 28–29) translated command as *Befehl*, implicitly keeping the term he found in Hobbes, Austin and Bentham. Marx maintained the original usage more clearly as *Kommando*.

Chapter 3 The Party-State and Political Commands

1   Fehér, Heller and Márkus (1983, 56, 108, 129) even speak of 'politocracy'. Lewin (2005, 349–50) postulates that this was really a 'non-party' system, due to the Communist Party's total bureaucratization. But this rests on a particular, a priori conception, according to which the party should have a capacity for mobilization, which was simply neither the case nor the goal. Calling it the 'vanguard party' (which brings together the best, most idealistic elements) (Lebowitz 2012, 69–72) is nothing more than wishful thinking. At best it takes what the 'party' thinks of itself, or cynically presents to society, at face value. Hilferding ([1940] 1947) was trenchant on the relation between bureaucracy and political power early on. For a more descriptive treatment, see Hazard (1980).

2   Note that Saint-Simon supported the rule of 'scientists, artists and artisans' (sided by proselytisers, just like himself), according to objective scientific 'principles', against the 'arbitrary decision of rulers'. The happiness of society was to be sought, a modern 'general principle of politics', against the treatment of nations as the 'patrimony' of rulers – who are mere 'parasites and dominators'. This would amount to a new form of sovereignty, in which the more capable would still govern, but with minimal functions. Despite an astonishingly similar rhetoric, we can hardly say that something similar happened in authoritarian collectivism.

3   For Lenin's thought, see Lih (2011). Surely, the tense relation between mostly short-term efficiency and democracy, especially in the long run, appears here immediately. The former prevailed; the latter disappeared, with long-lasting consequences.

4   These categories were paramount for Weber ([1921–22] 1980).

Chapter 4 The Law, Rights and the Judiciary

1   For an overview of Pashukanis's and Stuchka's ideas, see Sharlet 1974.

2   Also finding inspiration in Marx, I have proposed a rather different view, in which rights, law and citizenship – not contract – furnish the elementary elements of political modernity, though the modern state is soon introduced in the argument as a system of domination. See Domingues (2019a).

3   It is not relevant for my purposes here to estimate the reach of the repression, prisons, Gulags, torture, forced labour and famine produced by forced collectivization and murder by Stalin's regime. It was formidable in any case, although not as gigantic as most Western Cold War academics suggested (data for this period is discussed in Ellman (2002)). Mao's voluntarism led to catastrophes in China, but of a different nature, although repression was strong too and the Cultural Revolution left a legacy of intolerance. Pol Pot's and the Khmer Rouge's atrocities in Cambodia were far-reaching and have entailed much perplexity in the literature (Lavoix 2007). Authoritarianism and a lack of transparency buttress such disasters, which were not necessary but were not external to the dynamics of authoritarian collectivism either. Yet surely particularly the Cambodian genocide cannot be derived from this system, implying other, more obscure, elements.

Chapter 5 The Nomenklatura: Political Power and Social Privilege

1   China, Vietnam, Cuba, Angola and Mozambique were countries in which revolutionary armies had and sometimes still retain legitimacy and influence.

Chapter 6 Political Systems and Political Regimes

1   After Stalin considered this possibility in the 1930s and drew back in fear (Getty 1991; Lomb 2018), the topic disappeared from the Communist Party repertoire across the world, only to resurface more recently. Direct elections were, however, introduced.
2   At least Mao (1957) was aware of the contradictions (albeit, he thought, not 'antagonistic') between the party/state and the people.

Chapter 7 Developmental Trends

1   Lefort (1980a, 90) was, therefore, right when he stated that the Left had no proper theory of the state and, more broadly, of the political dimension, though his own definitions of 'the political', of totalitarianism and of the role of bureaucracy were wanting.

Chapter 8 Authoritarian Collectivism and Capitalism Today

1   Differences between imaginaries and practices – 'culture' – between East and West surely exist. But this is a problematic terrain, which the social sciences have had trouble crossing. This mars, for instance, Pye's ([1968] 1992; 1985) understanding of Chinese 'socialism', despite interesting occasional insights such as the centrality of morals in Chinese political discourse (which reappears in Vietnam, both stemming from Confucian traditions). Orientalism and an excessive effort to oppose Chinese views and behaviour to those with Western origins underpin his shortcomings. More interestingly, Børge (2000) mixes old Chinese traditions and 'real socialist' (Foucaultian) policies in the 'exemplary society'.
2   The core of the judicial system has survived the death of authoritarian collectivism in Eastern Europe (Markovits 2007) and is not necessarily negative in more open political circumstances, where limits to the state in relation to individuals and societal organizations exist.

Chapter 9 Socialism and Communism

1   The council tradition is doubtlessly powerful in this sense (see Mandel 1973 for a selection), but we should not reify it as the exclusive or even principal form of radical democracy. Nor should we view councils as superseding politics in what regards conflictive relations and decisions, though the separation between the political dimension and other differentiated dimensions of modernity is certainly not eternal. It is difficult to escape the imaginary grip of the 1871 Commune and the 1905/17 soviets.

REFERENCES

Adamczak, Birn (2018) *Beziehungweise Revolution: 1917, 1968 und kommende*. Frankfurt am Main: Suhrkamp.

Amos, Jennifer (2011) 'Embracing and contesting: The Soviet Union and the Universal Declaration of Human Rights, 1948–1958', in Hoffman, Stefan-Ludwig (ed.), *Human Rights in the Twentieth Century*. Cambridge: Cambridge University Press.

Anderson, Perry (2010) 'Two revolutions', *New Left Review*, no. 61: 59–95.

Andreas, Tony (2001) *From Afro-Stalinism to Petro-Diamond Capitalism*. Oxford: James Currey; Bloomington: Indiana University Press; and Lysaker: International African Institute.

Arato, Andrew (1993) *From Neo-Marxism to Democratic Theory: Essays on the Critical Theory of Soviet Societies*. Armonk, NY: M. E. Sharp.

——— (2019) 'Socialism and populism', *Constellations*, vol. 26(3): 464–74.

Arendt, Hannah ([1951] 1973) *The Origins of Totalitarianism*. San Diego, CA: Harvest/HJB.

Arnason, Johann P. (1993) *The Future That Failed: Origins and Destinies of the Soviet Model*. London: Routledge.

Aron, Raymon ([1965] 2017) *Démocratie et totalitarisme*. Paris: Gallimard.

Badiou, Alain (2003) *De quoi Sarkozy est-il le nom*. Paris: Lignes.

——— (2009) *L'Hypothèse communiste*. Paris: Lignes.

Bahro, Rudolf (1977) *Die Alternative: Zur Kritik des real existierenden Sozialismus*. Frankfurt am Main: Europäische Verlaganstalt.

Bahry, Donna, and Silver, Brian D. (1990) 'Soviet citizen participation on the eve of democratization', *American Political Science Review*, vol. 84(3): 821–47.

Bakunin, Michael ([1983] 1990) *Statism and Anarchy*. Cambridge, MA: Cambridge University Press.

Bertot Triana, Harold (2019) 'La constitución cubana de 2019 en perspectiva histórica e ideológica: aproximaciones a su sistema político-electoral', *Revista de derecho público*, no. 90: 11–40.

Bell, Daniel A. ([2015] 2016) *The China Model: Political Meritocracy and the Limits of Democracy*. Princeton, NJ: Princeton University Press.

——— (2008) *China's New Confucianism: Politics and Everyday Life*. Princeton, NJ: Princeton University Press.

Bell, Daniel A., and Pei, Wang (2020) *Just Hierarchy: Why Social Hierarchies Matter in China and the Rest of the World*. Princeton, NJ: Princeton University Press.

Bengelsdorf, Carollee (1994) *The Problem of Democracy in Cuba: Between Vision and Democracy*. Oxford: Oxford University Press.

Bernal, Martin (1981) 'Mao e la rivoluzione chinese', in Hobsbawm, Eric (ed.), *Storia del marxismo: Il marxismo nell'età della Terza Internazionale*. Turin: Einaudi.

Blackburn, Robin (1991) 'Fin de siècle: Socialism after the crash', *New Left Review*, no. 185: 5–66.

Børge, Bokken (2000) *The Exemplary Society: Human Improvement, Social Control, and the Dangers of Modernity in China*. Oxford: Oxford University Press.

Brenner, Philip, Rose Jiménez, Marguerite, Kirk, John M., and LeoGrande, William M. (2008) *A Contemporary Cuba Reader: Reinventing the Revolution*. Lanham, MD: Rowman & Littlefield.

Brunner, Georg (1966) 'Naturrechte und Sowjetideologie', *Berichte des Bundesinstituts für Ostwissenschaftliche und Internationale Studien*, no. 38: 1–19.

——— (1970) 'Zur Wirksamkeit der Grundrechte in Osteuropa', *Der Staat*, vol. 9(2): 187–222.

Bukharin, Nikolai (1925) *Historical Materialism: A System of Sociology*. Moscow: International Publishers.

Carlo, Antonio ([1971] 1975) 'La natura socio-economica dell'Urss', in *I Quaderni di Terzo Mondo*. Milan: Centro Studio Terzo Mondo.

Castoriadis, Cornelius ([1947] 1990) 'Sur la question de l'U.R.S.S. et la possibilité d'une troisième solution historique', in *La Société bureaucratique*. Paris: Christian Bourgeois.

——— ([1948] 1990) 'Phénoménologie de la conscience prolétarienne', in *La Société bureaucratique*. Paris: Christian Bourgeois.

——— ([1964] 1973) 'Le role de l'ideologie bolchevique dans la naissance de la bureaucratie', in *L'Expérience du mouvement ouvrier*, vol. 2. Proletariat et organisations. Paris: Union Générale d'Editions.

——— (1981) *Devant la guerre*. Paris: Fayard.

——— ([1987] 1990) 'L'Interlude Gorbathchov', in *La Société buraucratique*. Paris: Christian Bourgeois.

——— (1990) *La Société bureaucratique*. Paris: Christian Bourgeois. (The texts collected span from the mid-1940s to the late 1980s.)

Cohen, Stephen F. (1985) *Rethinking the Soviet Experience: Politics and History since 1917*. Oxford: Oxford University Press.

Creak, Simon, and Barney, Keith (2018) 'Conceptualizing party-state governance and rule in Laos', *Journal of Contemporary Asia*, vol. 48(5): 693–716.

Dean, Jodi (2016) *Crowds and Party*. London: Verso.

Dirlik, Arif (2005) *Marxism and the Chinese Revolution*. Lanham, MD: Rowman & Littlefield.

Dingxin, Zhao (2002) *The Power of Tiananmen: Society Relations and the 1989 Beijing Student Movement*, Chicago: University of Chicago Press.

Djilas, Milovan (1957) *The New Class: An Analysis of the Communist System*. London: Thames and Hudson.

Domingues, José Maurício (2000) *Social Creativity, Collective Subjectivity and Contemporary Modernity*. Harmondsworth: Macmillan; and New York: Saint Martin's Press (Palgrave).

——— ([2008] 2011) 'A Revolução Cubana entre o passado e o futuro', in *Teoria crítica e (semi)periferia*. Belo Horizonte: Editora UFMG.

——— ([2010] 2011) 'O confucionismo e a China hoje', in *Teoria crítica e (semi)periferia*. Belo Horizonte: Editora UFMG.

——— (2012a) *Global Modernity, Development, and Contemporary Civilization: Towards a Renewal of Critical Theory*. New York: Routledge.

——— (2012b) *Desarrollo, periferia y semiperiferia en la tercera fase de la modernidad global*. Buenos Aires: CLACSO.

—— (2017/2018) *Emancipation and History: The Return of Social Theory*. Leiden: Brill; and Chicago: Haymarket.

—— (2019a) *Critical Theory and Political Modernity*. New York: Palgrave Macmillan.

—— (2019b) 'Jacobinism, political modernity and global sociology', *Social Epistemology*, vol. 33(5): 422–32.

Drochon, Hugo (2020) 'Robert Michels, the iron law of oligarchy and dynamic democracy', *Constellations*, vol. 27(2): 185–98.

Economy, Elizabeth C. (2019) *The Third Revolution: Xi Jinping and the New Chinese State*. Oxford: Oxford University Press.

Ellman, Michael (2002) 'Soviet repression statistics: Some comments', *Europe-Asia Studies*, vol. 54(7): 1151–72.

Engels, Friedrich ([1878] 1975) *Herrn Eugen Dührings Umwälzung der Wissenschaft ('Anti-Dühring')*, in Marx, Karl and Engels, Friedrich, *Werke*, vol. 20. Berlin: Dietz.

Esherick, Joseph W. (1979) ' "On the restoration of capitalism": Mao and Marxist theory', *Modern China*, vol. 5(1): 41–77.

Fehér, Ferenc (1987) *The Frozen Revolution: An Essay on Jacobinism*. Cambridge: Cambridge University Press; and Paris: Maison des Sciences de l'Homme.

Fehér, Ferenc, Heller, Agnes, and Márkus, Györg (1983) *Dictatorship over Needs: An Analysis of Soviet Societies*. New York: Saint Martin's Press.

Friedrich, Carl J., and Brzezinski, Zbigniew ([1956] 1963) *Totalitarian Dictatorship and Autocracy*. New York: Praeger.

Gainsborough, Martin (2010) *Vietnam: Rethinking the State*. London: Zed.

Gallissot, René (1981) 'L'imperialismo e la questione nacionale e coloniale', in Hobsbawm, Eric (ed.), *Storia del marxismo: Il marxismo nell'età della Terza Internazionale*. Turin: Einaudi.

Garrick, John, and Chang Bennett, Yan (2018) ' "Xi Jinping Thought": Realisation of the Chinese dream of national rejuvenation?', *China Perspectives*, no. 2018/1–2: 99–105.

Getty, J. Archer (1991) 'State and society under Stalin: Constitutions and elections in the 1930s', *Slavic Review*, vol. 50(1): 18–35.

Giddens, Anthony (1985) *The Nation-State and Violence*. Cambridge: Polity.

Gillespie, John (2004) 'Concepts of law in Vietnam: Transforming statist socialism', Peerenboom, Randall (ed.), *Asian Conceptions of the Rule of Law: Theories and Implementation of Rule of Law in Twelve Countries, France and the US*. New York: Routledge.

Golan, Galia (1971) 'The road to reform', *Problems of Communism*, vol. XX: 11–21.

Gramsci, Antonio ([1929–35] 2001) *Quaderni del carcere*, vols 1–3. Turin: Einaudi.

Grigot, Ronald (2005) 'Learning from empire: Russia and the Soviet Union', in Calhoun, Craig, Cooper, Frederick and Moore, Kevin W. (eds), *Lessons of Empire: Imperial Histories and American Power*. New York: New Press.

Grzybowski, Kazimierz (1962) *Soviet Legal Institutions: Doctrines and SocialFunctions*. Ann Harbor: Michigan University Press.

Habermas, Jürgen (1981) *Theorie des kommunikativen Handelns*, vols 1–2. Frankfurt am Main: Suhrkamp.

Harding, Neil (ed.) (1984) *The State in Socialist Society*. Albany: State University of New York.

Hazard, John N. (1969) *Communists and Their Law: A Search for the Common Core of Marxian Socialist States*. Chicago: University of Chicago Press.

—— (1980) *The Soviet Political System*. Chicago: University of Chicago Press.

Hegedus, Andreas (1976) *Socialism and Bureaucracy*. London: Allison and Busby.

Hegel, Georg Wilhelm Friedrich ([1820] 1986) *Grundlinien der Philosophie des Rechts*, in *Werke*, vol. 7. Frankfurt am Main: Suhrkamp.

Hilferding, Rudolf ([1940] 1947) 'State, capitalism or totalitarian state economy', *Modern Review*, June: 266–71.

Hill, Ronald (1984) 'The "All-People's State" and "developed socialism"', in Harding, Neil (ed.), *The State in Socialist Society*. Albany: State University of New York.

Honneth, Axel (2015) *Die Idee des Sozialismus. Versuch einer Aktualisierung*. Frankfurt am Main: Suhrkamp.

Hough, Jerry F. (1977) *The Soviet Union and Social Science Theory*. Cambridge, MA: Harvard University Press.

Hualing, Fu, Gillespie, John, Nicholson, Pip, and Parlett, William, E. (eds) (2018) *Socialist Law in East Asia*. Cambridge: Cambridge University Press.

Huberman, Leo, and Sweezy, Paul M. (1969) *Socialism in Cuba*. New York: Monthly Review.

Ingram, David (2018) 'Jacobinism', *Krisis*, vol. 2: 88–90.

Izatt, Hillary J. (2010) 'Can North Korea develop? Developmental dictatorship versus the China reform model', *Asian Politics & Policy*, vol. 2(2): 175–95.

Jancar, Barbara W. (1971) *Czechoslovakia and the Absolute Monopoly of Power: A Study of Political Power in a Communist System*. New York: Praeger.

Jarausch, Konrad H. ([1988] 2012) 'Realer Sozialismus als Fürsorgediktatur: Zur begrifflichen Einordnung der DDR', *Historical Social Research*, supplement no. 24: 249–72.

Jünke, Christoph (2007) *Der lange Schatten des Stalinismus. Sozialismus und Demokratie Gestern und Heute*. Karsruhe: ISP.

Kapcia, Antoni (2021) *A Short History of Revolutionary Cuba: Revolution, Power, Authority and the State from 1959 to the Present Day*. London: Bloomsbury.

Kerkvliet, Benedict J. (2005) *The Power of Everyday Politics: How Vietnamese Peasants Transformed National Policy*. Ithaca, NY: Cornell University Press.

Kerkvliet, Benedict J., Tria, Heng, Russell H. K., and Koh, David W. H. (eds) (2003) *Getting Organized in Vietnam: Moving in and around the State*. Singapore: Institute of Southeast Asian Studies.

Kihl, Young Whan, and Kim, Hong Nack (eds) (2006) *North Korea: The Politics of Regime Survival*. Armonk, NY: East Gate.

Kornai, János (1992) *The Socialist System: The Political Economy of Socialism*. Oxford: Clarendon.

Korsch, Karl ([1919] 1969) 'Was ist Sozialisierung? Ein Programm des praktischen Sozialismus', in *Schriften zur Sozialisierug*. Frankfurt am Main: Europeanist Verlaganstaltt.

Kraus, Richard Curt (2012) *The Cultural Revolution: A Very Short Introduction*. New York: Oxford University Press.

Kuron, Jacek, and Modzelewski, Karol ([1966] 1982) *Solidarnosc: The Missing Link? The Classic Open Letter to the Party*. London: Book Marks.

Lander, Edgardo (2016) 'La implosión de la Venezuela rentista', *Cuadernos de la nueva política*, no. 1. Amsterdam: Transnational Institute.

——— (2020) *Crisis civilizatoria. Experiencias de los gobiernos progresistas y debates en la izquierda latinoamericana*. Guadalajara: Callas.

Lavoix, Hélène (2007) 'Cambodia', in *Online Encyclopedia of Mass Violence* (https://www.sciencespo.fr/mass-violence-war-massacre-resistance/en/document/cambodia), accessed 8 September 2021.

Lebowitz, Michael A. (2012) *The Contradictions of Real Socialism*. New York: Monthly Review.

Lefort, Claude ([1960] 1971) 'Qu'est-ce que la bureaucratie?', in *Elements d'une critique de la bureaucratie*. Paris: Droz.

——— (1980a) 'La logique totalitaire', in *L'Invention democratique*. Paris: Fayard.

——— (1980b) 'Staline et le stalinisme', in *L'Invention democratique*. Paris: Fayard.

Lenin, V. I. ([1904] 1964) *One Step Forward, Two Steps Back*, in *Collected Works*, vol. 7. Moscow: Progress.

——— ([1917] 1964) *The State and Revolution: A Marxist Theory of the State & the Tasks of the Proletariat in the Revolution*, in *Collected Works*, vol. 25. Moscow: Progress.

——— ([1921] 1965) 'Preliminary draft resolution of the Tenth Congress of the R.C.P. on party unity', in *Collected Works*, vol. 32. Moscow: Progress.

Lewin, Moshe ([1968] 2005) *Lenin's Last Struggle*. Ann Arbor: University of Michigan Press.

——— (2005) *The Soviet Century*. London: Verso.

Lih, Lars T. (2011) *Lenin*. London: Reaktion Books.

Lin, Chun (2006) *The Transformation of Chinese Socialism*. Durham, NC : Duke University Press.

Linden, Marcel van der (1992) *Western Marxism and the Soviet Union: A Survey of Critical Theories and Debates*. Leiden : Brill.

Lipset, Seymor M., and Bence, Gyorgy (1994) 'Anticipations of the failure of communism', *Theory and Society*, vol. 23(2): 163–210.

Lomb, Samantha (2018) *Stalin's Constitution: Soviet Participatory Politics and the Discussion of the 1936 Draft Constitution*. New York: Routledge.

London, Jonathan D. (ed.) (2014) *Politics in Contemporary Vietnam*. London: Palgrave.

Lopez Maya, Margarita (2016) *El ocaso del chavismo. Venezuela 2005–2015*. Caracas: Alfa.

Mandel, Ernest (1973) *Control ouvrier, conceils ouvriers, autogestion*. Paris: Maspero.

Mao Tse-Tung ([1934] n.d.a) 'Be concerned with the wellbeing of the masses, pay attention to the methods of work', in *Selected Works of Mao Tse-Tung*, vol. I. Peking: Foreign Language Press.

——— ([1957] n.d.a) 'On the correct handling of contradictions among the people', in *Selected Works of Mao Tse-Tung*, vol. I. Peking: Foreign Language Press.

——— ([1966-69] n.d.b) 'Directives regarding the Cultural Revolution', in *Selected Works of Mao Tse-Tung*, vol. IX. Peking: Foreign Language Press.

——— ([1967] 1977) *Critique of Soviet Economics*. New York: Monthly Review.

——— ([1970] n/d c) 'Twenty manifestations of bureaucracy', in *Selected Works of Mao Tse-Tung*, vol. IX. Peking: Foreign Language Press.

Marcuse, Herbert (1958) *Soviet Marxism*. New York: Columbia University Press.

Markovits, Inga (2007) 'The death of socialist law?', *Annual Review of Law and Social Science*, no. 3: 233–53.

Marx, Kark ([1843a] 1956) *Zu Kritik des hegelschen Rechtsphilosophie*, in Marx, Karl and Engels, Friedrich, *Werke*, vol. 1. Berlin: Dietz.

——— ([1843b] 1956) *Zur Juden Frage*, in Marx, Karl and Engels, Friedrich, *Werke*, vol. 1. Berlin: Dietz.

——— ([1859] 1971) 'Vorwort', in *Zur Kritik des politichen Ökonomie*, in Marx, Karl and Engels, Friedrich, *Werke*, vol. 13. Berlin: Dietz.

——— ([1867] 1962) *Das Kapital. Kritik der politischen Ökonomie*, vol. 1, in Marx, Karl and Engels, Friedrich, *Werke*, vol. 23. Berlin: Dietz.

——— ([1871] 1986) *The civil war in France*, in Marx, Karl and Engels, Friedrich, *Collected Works, 1870–1871*. London: Lawrence & Wishart.

——— ([1875] 1973) 'Kritik des Gothaer Programms', in Marx, Karl and Engels, Friedrich, *Werke*, vol. 18. Berlin: Dietz.

——— ([1894] 1964) *Das Kapital. Kritik der politischen Ökonomie*, vol. 3, in Marx, Karl and Engels, Friedrich, *Werke*, vol. 23. Berlin: Dietz.

Marx, Karl, and Engels, Friedrich ([1848] 1978) 'Manifest der kommunistischen Partei', in *Werke*, vol. 4. Berlin: Dietz.

Melotti, Umberto (1972) *Marx e il Terzo Mondo: Un schema multilineare della concezione marxiana dello sviluppo storico.* Milan: Il Saggiatore.

Merleau-Ponty, Maurice ([1947] 1951) *Humanisme et terreur.* Paris: Gallimard.

Merryman, John M. ([1977] 1985) *The Civil Law Tradition: An Introduction to the Legal Systems of Western Europe and Latin America.* Stanford, CA: Stanford University Press.

Michels, Robert ([1911] 1915) *Political Parties: A Sociological Study of the Oligarchical Tendencies of Modern Democracy.* New York: Hearter's International Library.

Mo Zhang (2010) 'The socialist legal system with Chinese characteristics: China's discourse for rule of law and a bitter experience', *Temple International & Comparative Law Journal,* vol. 24(1): 2011–22.

Mouzelis, Nicos (1993) 'Evolutionary democracy: Talcott Parsons and the collapse of Eastern European regimes', *Theory, Culture & Society,* vol. 19(1): 145–52.

Nathans, Benjamin (2011) 'Soviet rights-talk in the post-Stalin era', in Hoffman, Stefan-Ludwig (ed.), *Human Rights in the Twentieth Century.* Cambridge: Cambridge University Press.

Neumann, Franz ([1930] 1978) 'Die soziale Bedeutung der Grundrechte in der Weimarer Republik', in *Wirtschaft, Staat, Demokratie. Aufsätze 1930–1954.* Frankfurt am Main: Suhrkamp.

Nolan, Peter (1995) *China's Rise, Russia's Fall.* Harmondsworth: Macmillan; and New York: Saint Martin's Press.

Nove, Alec ([1983] 1991) *The Economics of Feasible Socialism Revisited.* London: HarperCollins.

O'Brien, Kevin J., and Han, Rongbin (2009) 'Path to democracy? Assessing village elections in China', *Journal of Contemporary China,* vol. 18(60): 359–78.

Pashukanis, Eugeny ([1924] 2017) *Law and Marxism: A General Theory.* London: Routledge.

——— ([1927] 1980) 'The Marxist theory of law and the construction of socialism', in *Selected Writings on Marxism and Law.* London: Routledge.

——— ([1932] 1980) 'The Marxist theory of law and the state', in *Selected Writings on Marxism and Law.* London: Routledge.

——— ([1936] 1980) 'State and law under socialism', in *Selected Writings on Marxism and Law.* London: Routledge.

Peerenboom, Randall (2002) *China's Long March towards the Rule of Law.* Cambridge: Cambridge University Press.

Pei, Wang (2017) 'Debates on political meritocracy in China: A historical perspective', *Philosophy and Public Issues (New series),* vol. 7(1): 53–71.

Pérez-Stable, Marifeli (1999) 'Caught in a contradiction: Cuban socialism between mobilization and normalization', *Comparative Politics,* vol. 32(1): 63–82.

Perry, Elizabeth J., and Goldman, Merle (eds) (2007) *Grassroots Political Reform in Contemporary China.* Cambridge, MA : Harvard University Press.

Pietcher, M. Anne (2002) *Transforming Mozambique: The Politics of Privatization, 1975–2000.* Cambridge: Cambridge University Press.

Piketty, Thomas, Li, Yang, and Zucman, Gabriel (2019) 'Capital accumulation, private property, and rising inequality in China, 1978–2015', *American Economic Review,* vol. 19(7): 2469–96.

Pye, Lucian W. ([1968] 1992) *The Spirit of Chinese Politics.* Cambridge, MA: MIT Press.

Pye, Lucian W. (1985) *Asian Conceptions of Power: The Cultural Dimensions of Authority.* Cambridge, MA: MIT Press.

Rabinowitch, Alexander (1976) *The Bolsheviks Come to Power: The Revolution of 1917 in Petrograd.* New York: W. W. Norton.

———— (2007) *The Bolsheviks in Power: The First Year of Soviet Rule in Petrograd*. Bloomington: Indiana University Press.

Raby, D. L. (2006) *Democracy and Revolution: Latin America and Socialism Today*. London: Pluto.

Rigby, T. H. ([1977] 1999) 'Stalinism and the mono-organizational society', in Tucker, Robert C. (ed.), *Stalinism: Essays in Historical Interpretation*. London: Routledge.

Rigby, T. H. (1964) 'Traditional, market and organizational societies and the USSR', *World Politics*, vol. 16(4): 539–57.

Rizzi, Bruno ([1939] 1976) *Le Collectivisme bureaucratique*. Paris: Champ Livre.

Runciman, W. G. (1995) 'The "Thriumph" of capitalism as a topic in the theory of social selection', *New Left Review*, no. 210: 33-47.

Saint-Simon, Claude-Henri de ([1820] 1967) *L'Organisateur*, Deuxième livraison, in *Ouevres complètes de Saint-Simon*, vol. 2. Paris: Anthropos.

Sakwa, Richard (2013) 'The Soviet collapse: contradictions and neo-modernization', *Journal of Eurasian Studies*, vol. 4(1): 65–77.

Samsónov, Dimitri P., and Días Torres, Isbel (2014) 'Las reformas cubanas: imaginarios, contestaciones y miradas críticas', *OSAL. Observatorio de América Latina*, año XIV (36): 17–46.

Sandle, Mark (2002) 'Brezhnev and developed socialism: The ideology of *zastoi*?', in Bacon, Edward and Sandle, Mark (eds), *Brezhnev Reconsidered*. Houndmills, Basingstoke: Palgrave Macmillan.

Schram, Stuart R. (1971) 'Mao Tse-Tung and the theory of permanent revolution, 1958–69', *China Quarterly*, vol. 9: 221–44.

Sharlet, Robert (1974) 'Pashukanis and the rise of Soviet Marxist jurisprudence, 1924–1930', *Soviet Union*, vol. 1(2): 103–21.

Shue, Vivienne (2004) 'Legitimacy crisis in China?', in Gries, Peter Hay, and Rosen, Stanley (eds), *State and Society in 21-Century China: Crisis, Contention and Legitimation*. New York: Routledge Curzon.

Sik, Ota (1971) 'The economic impact of socialism', *Problems of Communism*, vol. XX: 1–10.

Solomon, Susan (ed.) (1983) *Pluralism in the Soviet Union: Essays in Honour of H. Gordon Skilling*. London: Macmillan.

Stalin, Joseph V. ([1930] 1955) 'Political report of the central committee to the sixteenth congress of the C. P. S. U. (B.)', in *Works*, vol. 12. Moscow: Foreign Language Publishing House.

Stuchka (Stucka), Piet I. ([1919] 1988) 'Proletarian law', in *Selected Writings on Soviet Law and Marxism*. New York: Routledge.

———— ([1921] 1988) *Direito e luta de classes*. São Paulo: Acadêmica. (Only the first chapters of this book were translated into English, with apparently serious deficiencies, in Hazard, John N. (ed.), *Soviet Legal Philosophy*. Cambridge, MA: Harvard University Press.)

———— ([1924] 1988) 'Prefácio à 3ª. edição', in *Direito e luta de classes*. São Paulo: Acadêmica.

———— ([1925–1927] 1988) 'Law', in *Selected Writings on Soviet Law and Marxism*. New York: Routledge.

Sun, Yat-sen ([1924] 1999). 'The principle of democracy', *Contemporary Chinese Thought*, vol. 31(10): 64–68. (Extracted from *San Min Chu I – The Three Principles of the People*, a book of which a good edition is hard to find. It was translated into English originally in 1924.)

Sunkara, Bhaskar (2019) *The Socialist Manifesto: The Case for Radical Politics in an Age of Extreme Inequality*. London: Verso.

Sweezy, Paul (1980) *Post-Revolutionary Society*. New York: Monthly Review.

Szelenyi, Ivan and Szelenyi, Balazs (1994) 'Why socialism failed: Toward a theory of system breakdown – Causes of disintegration of East European state socialism', *Theory and Society*, vol. 23(2): 211-31.

Tapia, Luis, and Chavez, Marxa, (2020) *Producción y reproducción de desigualdades: organización social y poder político*. La Paz: CEDLA.

Tapia-Valdés, Jorge (1977) 'Cuba constitucional', *Nueva Sociedad*, no. 28: 87–101.

Tarifa, Fatos (1998) 'Legitimation crisis of state socialism: The Balkans vis-à-vis the Visegrád countries', *Balkanologie. Revue d'études pluridisciplinaries*, vol. 2(1): 1–12.

To, Phuc, Mahanty, Sango, and Wells-Dang, Andrew (2019) 'From "Land to the Tiller" to "New Landlords"? The debate over Vietnam's latest land reforms', *Land*, vol. 8: 1–19.

Trotsky, Leon ([1935] 1956) 'The workers' state, Thermidor and Bonapartism', *International Socialist Review*, vol. 17(3): 93–101.

———([1937] 2004) *The Revolution Betrayed*. New York: Pathfinder.

——— ([1938a] 1977) *The Transitional Program*. New York: Pathfinder.

——— ([1938b] 1973) *Their Morals and Ours*. New York: Pathfinder.

Tucker, Robert C. (1963) *The Soviet Political Mind: Studies in Stalinism and Post-Stalin Change*. London: Pall Mall.

——— (1999) 'Stalinism as revolution from above', in Tucker, Robert C. (ed.), *Stalinism: Essays in Historical Interpretation*. London: Routledge.

Urbinati, Nadia (2017) *Constitutioze italiana: artícolo 1*. Rome: Carocci.

Vyshinsky, Andrei Y. (1948) *The Law of the Soviet State*. New York: Macmillan.

Walles, Michael (1981) *Democratic Centralism: An Historical Commentary*. Manchester: Manchester University Press.

Wang Hui (2009) 'Preface to the English edition', in *The End of Revolution: China and the Limits of Modernity*. London: Verso.

Weber, Max ([1921–22] 1980) *Wirtschaft und Gesellschaft. Grundriss der verstehenden Soziologie*. Tübingen: J. C. B Mohr (Paul Siebeck).

——— ([1918] 1988) 'Der Sozialismus', in *Gesammelte Aufsätze zur Soziologie und Sozialpolitik*. Tübinger: J. C. B. Mohr (Paul Siebeck).

Xiapong, Cong (2014) ' "Ma Xiwu's way of judging": Villages, the masses and legal construction in revolutionary China in the 1940s', *China Journal*, vol. 72: 29–52.

Yu, Xingzhong (1989) 'Legal pragmatism in the People's Republic of China', *Journal of Chinese Law*, vol. 3(1): 29–51.

Yu-Jie, Chen (2019) 'China's challenge to the International Human Rights Regime', *NYU Journal of International Law and Politics*, vol. 51: 1179–222.

INDEX

Lightning Source UK Ltd.
Milton Keynes UK
UKHW012205211221
396039UK00001B/39